Meet My Father

by

Jim McAtee, Jr.

Ward:
God bless you
richly. It was a
pleasure having you with
us and making your
acquaintance.
Regards
& Godspeed
Jim

Companion Press
P.O. Box 310
Shippensburg, PA 17257-0310

"Good Stewards of the
Manifold Grace of God"

ISBN 1-56043-503-8

For Worldwide Distribution
Printed in the U.S.A.

Contents

Dedication

The immediate family always sees first hand the inner struggles of a person who is trying to be a man of God. They know of his times of uncertainty and lack of confidence, his inadequacies, moments of frustration and apparent helplessness. Despite all they know, they still love and support him as a father, friend and companion.

I affectionately dedicate this book to Bonnie, Shannon, Melissa and Libby.

Prologue

To most of the young people in that little white church in Warr Acres, Oklahoma, the summer of 1959 was an eventful year, a good ending to the decade. A sense of spiritual awakening possessed most of us. Consequently, we had developed some long-lasting relationships and had some never-to-be-forgotten experiences. Among those who were especially influenced by the events of that summer (as time would reveal) was J.D.

J.D. was the most serious member of our youth group and served as the conscience of the group. I always admired him for his dedication, although it seemed beyond my reach to copy.

One day J.D. accompanied me on a visit to the Wesley Hospital. Another of our young men, Robert, had been hospitalized with an eye injury, and we wanted to see how he was doing. We hadn't been there long when J.D. excused himself from the room. When he failed to return within a reasonable time, I decided to go looking for him.

I found him sitting on the steps of the hospital with his head buried between his knees, looking miserable.

"What happened?" I asked him. "Why did you go out like that?"

"Hospitals make me sick!" he replied.

I remembered that answer a few weeks later when J.D. stood to his feet in a Wednesday night testimony service in the church to say that God had called him to be a medical doctor. And he was serious. That fall he entered State College in Edmond, Oklahoma, and started on his quest for the will of God for his career. It would prove to be no easy task.

After three years at Central State, J.D. applied to medical school. Everyone was surprised when his application was rejected, even after two interviews. Because of what he believed God had told him, he was not discouraged and applied again the next year. This time he was accepted and went on to finish his training and become a most successful doctor.

For many years, I thought how wonderful it would be to know God in the depth and with the intimacy with which my friend J.D. knew Him. His intimate knowledge of God and God's will drove him on in the face of impossible odds to accomplish the very best in his life. How I admired that!

Gradually, over time, the heavenly Father began to reveal Himself to me, and I came to understand that He is actually anxious to reveal Himself to each of us—if we can only reach out in faith to Him. It was in this way that I discovered the foundational truths of this book. Come, let me introduce you to my Father.

Introduction

"And you, my son Solomon, acknowledge the God of your father, and serve him with wholehearted devotion and with a willing mind, for the Lord searches every heart and understands every motive behind the thoughts. If you seek him, he will be found by you; but if you forsake him, he will reject you forever."

1 Chronicles 28:9

What wonderful advice for a father to give his son!

When I graduated from high school, I felt that I was ready for the adult world. One day I approached my father and asked him what advice he could give me for my future.

Dad was not a highly educated man. He grew up in the little town of Brownstown in Southwest Arkansas and completed only the sixth grade. He couldn't continue his education because he needed to work and help his father with the support of the family (there were six brothers and sisters). So manhood was thrust upon him at an early age; and, in response, he became a fur trader.

Early every Monday morning he left home and went to spend the week in a lean-to by the river. His companions there were a shotgun, his favorite coon dog and some animal traps. He set the traps along the river banks and tended them daily. When an animal was captured, he would clean and stretch the hide. By weeks end, he had a collection of hides to take to market on Saturday morning. Saturday nights and Sundays were spent with the family.

This experience made my father a very wise and understanding person. He answered my question like this: "Son, all I can tell you is that there are no short-cuts in this life. Some people seem to make it through life on minimal effort, but to really succeed and become a person of integrity and respect, there are no short cuts." I believed him, and I never forgot his words.

David was a unique father. He went through all the cycles of life: success and failure, heartache and victory. When he won battles against the enemy, he won the praises of his people. But he also failed miserably at times and became an embarrassment to himself, to his family, and to God.

Because of David's personal failures, he had to forfeit the privilege of building a temple for God and for his people in Jerusalem. He lived with some deep regrets, but he refused to let his past keep him defeated. It was because of his refusal to remain in a defeated state of mind, that God said of him:

> *'I have found David son of Jesse a man after my own heart; he will do everything I want him to do.'*
>
> Acts 13:22 (NIV)

Like most of us, David tried to guide his son Solomon into the right paths so that he would not have to make the same mistakes and suffer the same consequences as his father. David was not being hypocritical when he offered this advice. He had gotten his own life under control. He was sorry for his former indiscretions. He understood his mistakes and was deeply sorrowful. He simply did not want Solomon to miss God's best for his life.

Speaking to your children is not always easy, and most parents are embarrassed to do it, but it has to be done. What we have learned through years in unproductive pursuits must be passed along to the next generations, lest they repeat our mistakes. How can we do less?

As Christians, we must continually assess our walk with the Lord. This requires us to examine carefully some of our failures, and we all have them. None of us are perfect. Our willingness to face our weaknesses and failures and to go on to a deeper knowledge of the Father will determine our future role in the Body of

Christ. We must be honest with ourselves and with God.

With all that life has brought us, I have reached the conclusion that David had a great secret: Of all that I would like to accomplish in life, nothing is more important than for me to sincerely acknowledge God and to serve Him with wholehearted devotion and with a willing mind...and to make Him known to others so that they may do the same.

In order to obey this Scriptural admonition, we need to understand God. What is He like? What are the qualities that make Him worthy of man's deepest devotion? Everything that we can learn about Him will help us in our quest. It was for this reason that the Apostle Paul declared to the Philippians:

> *I want to know Christ and the power of his resurrection and the fellowship of sharing in his sufferings, becoming like him in his death.*
>
> Philippians 3:10

In the following chapters, I want to help you to know God in a very intimate way. I want to let the Scriptures paint a verbal picture of Him. I want us to look into His eyes, to feel the touch of His hand, and to witness the sensitivity of His hearing.

Picturing God in human terms (with hands, eyes, ears, heart, etc.) is very controversial. Many theologians warn against it. "*God is a Spirit*" (John 4:24,

KJV). *"No man hath seen God at any time"* (John 1:18). How can God be compared to a man?

I certainly don't want to raise yet another controversy in your spiritual life. What I want to do is use God's "physical features" in a metaphorical sense that suggests a much deeper spiritual meaning. The Bible does this very thing, so we are safe in doing it.

If this book can help you to draw closer to the Father, to understand Him better, to experience His goodness in some way, I shall be pleased; and to Him be all the glory, both now and forevermore.

Jim McAtee, Jr.
Sanford, Maine

Chapter 1

His All-Seeing EYES

But Noah found favor in the EYES of the Lord.
Genesis 6:8

We have a wonderful group of young people in our church. Not long ago I overheard one of our teenagers describing her boyfriend. She might have been describing the lines of a vintage 1955 Chevrolet. She had studied every line of his facial features as carefully as an artist about to capture an image on canvas, the nose, the eyes, the mouth, the hair etc. His smile meant everything to her, and she could describe it in detail.

Nothing was mentioned about the young man's character. The wonderful thing about the facial features of the Lord is that they speak to us of His character. When we look into His EYES, we catch a glimpse of Who He really is, and we are never the same again.

God's EYES are first mentioned in the book of Genesis, that book of beginnings. Thus, from the very beginning of His dealings with mankind, God has made it plain that He sees everything and knows everything. Nothing escapes Him. His EYES beheld Adam and Eve, Cain and Abel, Enoch and Methuselah. Much of what God saw displeased Him and brought forth His wrath upon creation; But Noah was a man who sought God and found grace (favor) in God's EYES. The same cannot be said for many others:

> *When men began to increase in number on the earth and daughters were born to them, the sons of God saw that the daughters of men were beautiful, and they married any of them they chose.*
>
> Genesis 6:1-2

Part of the fallout from the sin of Adam and Eve was man's seeming insistence on selecting an unbelieving mate. Instead of choosing someone on the same spiritual plane, someone that feared God and wanted to obey Him, men began to take unbelieving wives, mixing light with darkness. Therefore, as the population of the world steadily increased, so did the problems that man faced.

> *Then the Lord said, "My Spirit will not contend with man forever, for he is mortal; his days will be a hundred and twenty years."*
>
> Genesis 6:3

The Living Bible says: "I will give him 120 years to change his ways." But man was willful and reluctant to change his ways; and "the Lord SAW."

The Lord SAW how great man's wickedness on the earth had become, and that every inclination of the thoughts of his heart was only evil all the time.
Genesis 6:5

God was looking for a change in the attitude of man. He was eagerly awaiting some response to His warning. Would man turn to Him? What He saw saddened His heart. He saw not only an increase in man's wickedness, but that "every inclination the thoughts of his heart was only evil all the time." The result was that "the Lord was grieved" (Genesis 6:6).

It is hard for us to imagine what God was feeling. The crowning glory of His creation had turned against Him. He had created man for fellowship, making him in His own image, only to have him become His enemy. The highest order of life had become disgraced through sin and disobedience. You would have been "grieved" too.

So the Lord said, "I will wipe mankind, whom I have created, from the face of the earth—men and animals, and creatures that move along the ground, and birds of the air—for I am grieved that I have made them."
Genesis 6:7

It was in the midst of all this sadness and loss that "Noah found grace in the EYES of the Lord" (KJV). The glorious world that God had created was now spoiled with wickedness. As His EYES roamed the entire earth, most of what He saw only brought further sadness to His heart. This angered God and caused Him to want to punish man.

Thank God that His EYES are all-seeing and that nothing escapes Him. For there was one man who was still trying to serve God. He loved God so much that he felt very badly about what people around him were doing. Being in the minority, he felt very alone and insignificant. How could he stand against the flood of evil around him? How could he convince people that God was real and deserving of their devotion?

God saw the desire of Noah's heart, and "Noah found favor in the EYES of the Lord." Through the miracle of the Ark, Noah and all his family were saved from the judgment that came upon the whole earth.

The Human EYE

The EYE is a marvelous thing. Our human EYE can be likened to a remarkable camera. It can aim and focus in half a second. Its aperture (lens opening) can adjust in even less time than that. The "color film" on which the EYE records the image it perceives is stereoscopic and self-renewing after every exposure. The developing time of the film is measured in milliseconds. What a marvelous creation the EYE is!

Our EYES are so important to us. Scientists tell us that what we see with our EYES stays with us more than what we hear with our ears. When we rely on verbalization alone to communicate, an estimated 90% of a message is misinterpreted or forgotten entirely.

We retain only about 10% of what we hear. But when something visual is used for communication, our retention makes a great leap.

What we see in another person's EYES is also revealing. The EYES are very expressive. Often we look to them to determine what a person is thinking or feeling. According to an article in National Geographic News, Chinese Jade sellers watch a buyers EYES to judge whether or not he will pay a high price for a specimen. Confirming this cunning practice, psychologists have established that the pupils of a person's EYES widen when he is looking at something that pleases him. (1)

Dogs are said to have the ability to judge from the expression of the masters EYES whether he is about to scold or reward them.

The EYE of God

God's EYES are so much more powerful than the human eye. His EYES are divine and speak to us of His multifaceted character.

The phrase, the EYES of the Lord, comes from the Hebrew word *'ayin*. It is used in Scripture in several ways. It expresses "knowledge, character, attitude, inclination, opinion, passion and response." (2)

His EYES are for judgment:

God uses His EYES for making an evaluation of man. His EYES are "open to all the ways of men."

O great and powerful God, whose name is the Lord Almighty, great are your purposes and mighty are your deeds. Your EYES are open to all the ways of men; you reward everyone according to his conduct and as his deeds deserve.

Jeremiah 32:18-19

God is looking for proof of man's faithfulness toward Him. He knows exactly what He is looking for. David declared:

The Lord has rewarded me according to my righteousness, according to my cleanness IN HIS SIGHT.

2 Samuel 22:25

God spoke through Ezekiel:

And mine EYE shall not spare thee, neither will I have pity: but I will recompense thy ways upon thee, and thy abominations shall be in the midst of thee: and ye shall know that I am the Lord.

Ezekiel 7:4 (KJV)

God does not judge us by the sin in our lives. He judges us according to whether or not we have allowed Him to make us righteous. He is against "*the sinful.*"

"Surely the EYES of the Sovereign Lord are on the sinful kingdom. I will destroy it from the face of the earth."

Amos 9:8

But God does not delight in judgment. He is a loving God, a truth which His EYES clearly reveal.

His EYES reveal His pleasure in His children:

God delights in His children and has classified us as *"precious."* The ancient patriarch Job declared in the midst of his horrendous trials:

> *He tunnels through the rock; his EYES see all its treasures.*
>
> Job 28:10

Several times in the Old Testament God referred to His saints as *"the apple of His EYE"* meaning that which brings Him pleasure (Deuteronomy 32:10, Psalms 17:8, Zechariah 2:8).

His EYES reveal His longing for man:

When you long for someone special, you never stop thinking of that person. You have a constant anticipation of the response you expect from them.

> *For the EYES of the Lord range throughout the earth to strengthen those whose hearts are fully committed to him.*
>
> 2 Chronicles 16:9

As God's EYES range throughout the earth, they are expressing His longing for some response from His most prized creation. It is impossible for us to comprehend the depth of His longing. He never takes His EYES off us.

But the EYES of the Lord are on those who fear him, on those whose hope is in his unfailing love.

Psalms 33:18

His EYES reveal His devotion to man:

Before the formation of the heavens and the earth, God's devotion to man was determined. To prove His devotion, He would give His most Prized Possession, His only begotten Son, as a sacrifice for man's sin. What greater expression of His devotion could we demand? God loves man. You can see it in His EYES.

His EYES are caring:

When Moses was on the back side of the desert keeping the flocks of his father-in-law, God SAW him. He sent an angel to speak to Moses in a flame of fire out of a burning bush. The bush caught Moses' attention and drew him out of the well of despair into which he had fallen since his exile from Egypt.

When the Lord SAW that he had gone over to look, God called to him from within the bush, "Moses! Moses!" And Moses said, "Here I am. Do not come any closer," God said. "Take off your sandals, for the place where you are standing is holy ground." Then he said, "I am the God of your father, the God of Abraham, the God of Isaac and the God of Jacob." At this, Moses hid his face, because he was afraid to look at God. The Lord said, "I have indeed SEEN the misery of my people in Egypt. I have heard them crying out because of their slave drivers, and I am concerned about their suffering. So I have come down to rescue them from the hand of the Egyptians and to bring them up out of that land into a good and spacious land, a land flowing with milk and honey—the home of the Canaanites, Hittites, Amorites, Perizzites, Hivites and Jebusites."

Exodus 3:4-8

Not only had God seen Moses plight on the back side of the desert. He had also seen the suffering of His people in Egypt and had devised a plan to deliver them and to take them into a good land which He had prepared.

His EYES are strong:

You save the humble, but your EYES are on the haughty to bring them low.

2 Samuel 22:28

God's EYES look favorably on the sensitive heart that is searching for Him. He is always ready to rescue the afflicted and needy. In the same way, His EYES behold the proud and disobedient and are strong to perform His will upon those who have made themselves His enemies.

His EYES are constant:

The EYES of the Lord are on the righteous and his ears are attentive to their cry;

Psalms 34:15

This is just as much true today as it was thousands of years ago. His EYES are constant.

His EYES are eternal:

Unlike human EYES, God's EYES don't grow dim with age. Because He is ageless, His EYES are ageless. He needs no magnifying glass and no special lighting to read by.

> *Your EYES saw my substance, being yet unformed. And in Your book they all were written, The days fashioned for me, When as yet there were none of them.*
>
> Psalms 139:16 (NKJV)

You...scheduled each day of my life before I began to breathe. Every day was recorded in Your Book.

Psalms 139:16 (The Living Bible)

His EYES saw us before our body had taken shape in the womb. Everything about us was already written in His book. His EYES are eternal.

In many ways, Noah's time can be compared to our own. He found himself living in the midst of a wicked and perverse generation. He was surrounded by an incomprehensible jumble of pressures, by unfairness and unjustness on every hand. The very atmosphere was threatening, and it seemed to be deteriorating by the minute. He probably asked himself many times:

"Where will all this end?"

"Doesn't anyone care?"

"Why doesn't someone do something?"

"Can't God see me in my despairing situation?"

The answer, of course, soon became apparent. YES! God does SEE. He does know. His EYES constantly roam the earth. Nothing escapes Him. He is all-seeing. He knew Noah's heart and *"Noah found grace [Divine favor and acceptance] in the EYES of the Lord."*

These truths concerning God's EYES have not changed since Bible days. His EYES are still strong, eternal and constant. Don't try to escape EYE contact with the God of the Universe. Allow His EYES to meet yours. In them you will see the expression of His longing for YOU, His devotion to YOU, and His desire for YOU.

Chapter 2

His Ever-Listening EARS

I love the Lord, for he HEARD my voice; he HEARD my cry for mercy. Because he turned his EAR to me, I will call on him as long as I live. The cords of death entangled me, the anguish of the grave came upon me; I was overcome by trouble and sorrow. Then I called on the name of the Lord: "O Lord, save me!"

Psalms 116:1-4

What a wonderful God we serve! He has EARS to HEAR our every cry.

One day the title of an Ann Lander's column in the newspaper caught my eye. **"Ministers' Wives Need Counseling Too,"** it proclaimed. I decided to read on.

Dear Ann Landers:

I am married to a minister in North Carolina. Please do not print the name of the city. He would kill me.

The problem is my husband. Whenever I ask him to do something that he doesn't want to do, he says, "I spoke to God and He said I shouldn't do it." I wish the man had the decency to say straight out that he doesn't want to do something instead of laying it on the back of the Lord.

I haven't seen my mother in three years. I told my husband that I wanted to go visit her. Well, he prayed over it and God told him this wasn't the right time. It was the right time, however, for him to treat fifteen friends to lunch in a nice restaurant while I stayed home and cooked for twenty-two Girl Scouts.

God tells my husband when to play golf and when to go fishing. He has also instructed him to go to some beautiful vacation spots (alone) so he can meditate and pray. I know I need counseling, but a minister's wife isn't supposed to have problems and I'm afraid that it might reflect poorly on my husband if I went for help. In this town, everybody knows everybody else's business.

Just writing this letter has made me feel better. Thanks for being there. And, please tell me what to do, Ann.

(signed, Stymied and Stuck in a no-name place.)

Ann Landers offered the following reply:

Dear Stymied and Stuck,

Get some counseling, woman! Ministers' wives need it just as much (if not more) than other wives. Make plans at once to visit your mother. Tell your husband you need it just as much as (if not more than) other wives.

Tell your husband you wrote to me and I consulted the Lord. The Lord quoted the commandment that says:

"Honor thy Father and thy Mother" and I decided that you should honor your mother with a visit right away.

The article is humorous, but it raises some interesting questions. This minister in question claimed to have an inside track to God. Is that possible? Well, not really. God does have EARS to HEAR, and He is ready and willing to HEAR the cry of all those who call upon Him. Not everyone, however, is aware of the power of God's ever-listening EARS.

David gives as one of the reasons he loved the Lord the fact that God HEARD his prayer. Isn't it wonderful to have someone to call upon in time of need! Isn't it wonderful to know that He is always attentive and always responsive! What a wonderful Father!

David was not free of problems. He had his share. His secret, however, was that he knew what to do in time of trouble. He knew Who to call upon.

> *In my distress I called to the Lord; I called out to my God. From his temple he HEARD my voice; my cry came to his EARS.*
>
> 2 Samuel 22:7

The Human Ear

The EAR is a fascinating organ. Next to being blind, deafness is perhaps man's most dreaded fear. There are many forms of deafness, some more serious than others. In one medically recognized form of deafness, the person affected is able to HEAR everything except words. In such cases, the ear may be so perfect that it can HEAR and appreciate the tick of a watch or the sound of a bird; but, due to an unusual injury to the HEARING mechanism, spoken words are unintelligible.

Most of us really appreciate our EARS and would be lost without them. They seem most important to us during times of crisis. When a news bulletin is flashed on the television screen, we become "all EARS." We want to know exactly what has happened. We trust our EARS to bring the news of important world events to attention of our brains and thought processes.

To some, it is a frightening idea that, with the passage of time, our HEARING begins to fade. Some older people need a HEARING aid to enhance their HEARING. Others, even less fortunate, lose the function of the EAR completely.

The EAR is important to us because it is the channel through which we learn most everything. As the old saying goes: *"Talk, and you say what you already know. BUT listen and you will learn something new."*

Not only do we need EARS to learn. We need EARS to communicate with others. To entertain some people, all you have to do is listen. What would we do without this wonderful ability?

If we are to believe some studies in psychology, it is possible to judge a person's personality by the shape and size of his or her EARS. (3)

For example, large, rounded EARS supposedly reveal a strong and ambitious nature concerned about truth and ideals. Excessively large and fleshly EARS supposedly point to a proud and pretentious nature.

Small EARS (these studies purport) belong to careful and prudent people who have the gift of willpower and perseverance. They are alleged to be evidence of a constantly wakeful intelligence. Small EARS are not likely to miss a sound or an opportunity (according to the authors of the study).

Oval EARS, when they are well-formed, show wisdom (we are told). A person with oval EARS loves to study and has a desire for perfection (so they say).

Cauliflower-shaped or otherwise not well-formed EARS are the hallmark of frustrated, vulgar people void of both charm and ideas (they say).

If the two EARS are different, as is often the case, these studies allege that this difference has an important meaning, that: If the right ear is larger than the left, the person will act in instinctive ways. Fantasy has a stronger influence in this person than reason. If the left ear is the larger one, the person is the cerebral type who never decides things casually.

God's EARS

Does God have EARS in the human sense? Probably not. But His EARS are more powerful and functional than mere human EARS. His EARS are sensitive, accurate, receptive, and compassionate.

The Hebrew word used to speak of God's EARS is *'ozen*. It simply means: *to give audience unto.* (4)

It is always fascinating to know someone who has had an audience with a famous personality—for whatever reason. The stories people tell about speaking with a president or a pope or a sports hero or a movie star have always generated a lot of interest. Photos taken during these occasions are prized mementos.

A good friend of mine, because of his distinguished military career, has been invited to the White House on several occasions to attend the President's Christmas Party. When he got the first invitation, he discussed with his family what was proper procedure and etiquette while in the company of the First Family, explaining to his family what would be expected of them.

When the magic night arrived, they found themselves standing in the receiving line anxiously awaiting their turn to shake hands with President and Mrs. Ronald Reagan. My friend would go first; then he would turn and take pictures of his family as they shook hands with the President.

After his turn came, he got his camera focused and watched as his wife approached the President and extended her right hand. Then, in dismay, he saw her left arm go up and around the President's neck. For a moment he was paralyzed with fear, wondering what would be the ramifications of this infraction of protocol. At home he chided his wife, expressing his disbelief that she had embraced the President.

She wasn't impressed. "My dear," she answered, "You didn't think I was going to get that close to the President of the United States and blow the opportunity to hug him, did you? Looking at the President in their photo. He loved it." And she was right.

Which of us would not be thrilled to have the ear of the President of the United States? It would be a great temptation not to abuse that privilege. Someone to listen to our problems ranks right up there with someone with loving arms who can comfort us in times of stress. An audience with an important person is a memorable experience.

Yet, when we think about it, God has given us that privilege. We can approach the Creator of the Universe and not be limited by man's protocol. We have God's EAR. He is interested in our problems. He has time to listen to our concerns.

David found that fact to be one of the most wonderful things about his relationship with God. *"I love the Lord,"* he said *"for he HEARD my voice; he HEARD my cry for mercy. Because he turned his EAR to me..."* Nothing could be more wonderful!

God is a good listener. He listens intelligently, contentedly, discerningly, with perception and understanding. He HEARS everything that His children tell Him. And sometimes, when we don't even understand the problem and cannot know what to ask for, He is one step ahead of us. He can discern what we are trying to say. No one needs to feel inadequate to talk to God. He looks beyond the words we speak and reads our hearts.

God bends down to HEAR and understand us, much as we might bend down to HEAR the words of a toddler. David said: "*...he hath inclined his EAR unto me*" (KJV). That word *incline* in the original was *natah* which means *to stretch out or extend yourself toward someone.* God has extended Himself to us so that He can HEAR our faintest cry. He bends down to our level so that He won't miss any of what we are trying to say.

Many adults are discourteous to toddlers. They stretch their little necks, nearly losing their balance, looking awkwardly up at us to tell us something important. And many of us barely notice their efforts.

We are just as awkward as toddlers in the presence of God. We are often incapable of expressing ourselves correctly. Yet He is ever respectful of our needs. He bends low toward us and stretches His EAR to HEAR every single word we want to say to Him. He doesn't miss a thing.

God's EARS are sensitive. He can HEAR sounds even before they are made. He HEARS prayers even before they are offered up to Him.

> *Before they call I will answer; while they are still speaking I will HEAR.*
>
> Isaiah 65:24

> *Your Father knows what you need before you ask him.*
>
> Matthew 6:8

He HEARS the cry of the righteous.

He HEARS the prayer of the righteous.

Proverbs 15:29

He HEARS the cry of the needy.

The Lord HEARS the needy and does not despise his captive people.

Psalms 69:33

Some people would just like to forget the needy. But God is eager to help them. He HEARS their cry. It makes no difference to Him if they are needy in a physical sense or in a spiritual sense. He wants to help both equally. "*Needy*" means lacking something vital, and God cannot rest when one of His children is lacking something vital. He HEARS their cry—when no one else does.

He HEARS the cry of the afflicted.

He HEARS the cry of the afflicted.

Job 34:28 (NKJV)

The "*afflicted*" are people who have been humbled by the force of undue circumstances, often by unfair labor practices. God HEARS their cry. Hard work is pleasing to the Lord, but labor abuse is another thing.

Then we cried out to the Lord, the God of our fathers, and the Lord HEARD our voice and saw our misery, toil and oppression.

Deuteronomy 26:7

Look! The wages you failed to pay the workmen who mowed your fields are crying out against you. The cries of the harvesters have reached the EARS of the Lord Almighty.

James 5:4

He HEARS the cry of those who are trying to escape from bondage.

"You saw the suffering of our forefathers in Egypt; you HEARD their cry at the Red Sea. You sent miraculous signs and wonders against Pharaoh, against all his officials and all the people of his land, for you knew how arrogantly the Egyptians treated them. You made a name for yourself, which remains to this day."

Nehemiah 9:9-10

He HEARS prayers of dedication.

The Lord said to him: "I have HEARD the prayer and plea you have made before me; I have consecrated this temple, which you have built, by putting my Name there forever. My eyes and my heart will always be there."

1 Kings 9:3

The best insurance policy on your home is a prayer of dedication unto the Lord.

He HEARS prayers of faith.

The Lord HEARD Elijah's cry, and the boy's life returned to him, and he lived.

1 Kings 17:22

Therefore confess your sins to each other and pray for each other so that you may be healed. The prayer of a righteous man is powerful and effective.

James 5:16

He HEARS the voice of the humble and tender-hearted.

"Because your heart was tender, and you humbled yourself before God when you HEARD His words against this place and against its inhabitants, and you humbled yourself before Me, and you tore your clothes and wept before Me, I also have HEARD you," says the Lord.

2 Chronicles 34:27 (NKJV)

He HEARS in His appointed time.

Thus says the Lord: "In an acceptable time I have HEARD You, and in the day of salvation I have helped You; I will preserve You and give You as a covenant to the people, to restore the earth, to cause them to inherit the desolate heritages;"

Isaiah 49:8 (NKJV)

How impatient we get with God! How alarmed we get when He is silent! It may be that we are simply awaiting His time.

He HEARS that which threatens His children.

"Now, Lord, consider their threats and enable your servants to speak your word with great boldness. Stretch out your hand to heal and perform miraculous

signs and wonders through the name of your holy servant Jesus."

After they prayed, the place where they were meeting was shaken. And they were all filled with the Holy Spirit and spoke the word of God boldly.

Acts 4:29-31

Christianity functions best in times of adversity; and our weaknesses are often discovered during times of abundance and comfort. When God sees that His children are threatened in any way, He acts quickly and decisively.

He HEARS when we pray for the members of our family.

"Believe in the Lord Jesus, and you will be saved—you and your household."

Acts 16:31

When the jailer charged with keeping Paul and Silas in the prison of Philippi saw that they were loose because of the effects of an earthquake, he was about to kill himself. But Paul and Silas were still there. They had not bothered to escape. When the man saw that, he marveled and asked them what he had to do to be saved too. Paul's answer was that believing produces salvation for us and for our family members as well.

These words proved to be true. When the jailer had attended to the apostles' wounds, *"he and all his family were baptized"* (Acts 16:33).

He HEARS—when we pray according to His will.

This is the confidence we have in approaching God: that if we ask anything according to his will, he HEARS us.

1 John 5:14

Yes, God HEARS, and because He is such a great and benevolent God, He can proclaim to us.

'Call to me and I will answer you and tell you great and unsearchable things you do not know.'

Jeremiah 33:3

There are times, however, when God chooses not to HEAR. The Bible gives us several examples.

When spouses are not living in harmony, God chooses not to HEAR their prayers.

Husbands, in the same way be considerate as you live with your wives, and treat them with respect as the weaker partner and as heirs with you of the gracious gift of life, so that nothing will hinder your prayers.

1 Peter 3:7

Husbands and wives who fail to show respect for one another are hindering the answer to their prayers. The minister in the Ann Lander's column was sure that God was HEARING his prayer. But he was not HEARING the legitimate concerns of his wife. This kind of attitude closes the heavens.

A person who is demanding, dissatisfied, unfulfilled, non-committed, or unthankful, etc., will suddenly find that God is deaf. Family members may feel obligated to respond to demonstrations of selfishness, but God does not.

As we have seen, when men and women choose not to repent of their sin and to love God, He chooses not to HEAR their prayers.

We know that God does not listen to sinners. He listens to the godly man who does his will.

John 9:31

God chooses not to HEAR the prayer of hypocrites.

If I had cherished sin in my heart, the Lord would not have listened.

Psalms 66:18

The insincere, the half-hearted and the part-time confessor of faith are wasting their time when they try get God to HEAR their phony prayers. When they get serious, God is more than ready to listen.

His EARS never get tired of the voice of all those who love Him.

Surely the arm of the Lord is not too short to save, nor his EAR too dull to HEAR.

Isaiah 59:1

Are you enjoying the friendship and fellowship of my Father in this capacity? You can. Take Him at His Word today. Trust His promises. Call to Him and you will see that He has all the time in the world to listen to you.

Chapter 3

His Radiant FACE

So Jacob was left alone, and a man wrestled with him till daybreak. When the man saw that he could not overpower him, he touched the socket of Jacob's hip so that his hip was wrenched as he wrestled with the man. Then the man said, "Let me go, for it is daybreak."
But Jacob replied, "I will not let you go unless you bless me."
The man asked him, "What is your name?"
"Jacob," he answered.
Then the man said, "Your name will no longer be Jacob, but Israel, because you have struggled with God and with men and have overcome."
Jacob said, "Please tell me your name."
But he replied, "Why do you ask my name?" Then he blessed him there. So Jacob called the place Peniel, saying, "It is because I saw God FACE to FACE, and yet my life was spared."

Genesis 32:24-30

The songwriter R.H. Cornelius, expressed the longing of every true believer in His classic hymn, *"Oh I Want To See Him."*

Oh I Want To See Him

As I journey through the land, singing as I go,
Pointing souls to Calvary—To the Crimson flow.
Many arrows pierce my soul; from without, within,
But my Lord leads me on, through Him I must win.

When in service for my Lord, dark may be the night,
But I'll cling more close to Him, He will give me light.
Satan's snares may vex my soul, turn my thoughts aside;
But my Lord goes ahead, leads whate'er be-tide.

When in valleys low I look tow'rd the mountain height,
And behold my Saviour there, leading in the fight.
With a tender hand outstretched tow'rd the valley low,
Guiding me, I can see, as I onward go.

When before me billows rise from the mighty deep,
Then my Lord directs my bark; He doth safely keep,
And He leads me gently on through this world below;
He's a real Friend to me, O I love him so.

CHORUS:

Oh I want to see Him, look upon His FACE,
There to sing forever of His saving grace;
On the streets of Glory let me lift my voice;
Cares all past, home at last, ever to rejoice. (5)

This well-known chorus still moves us after so many years. One can find great consolation in these words. It is easy to see that they are God-inspired. But, although we treasure many of our old hymns, there is a negative side to always looking to see Christ in some future moment. Too many are missing the benefits of living in His presence now.

I take issue with those who say that life here on earth is just a bore and that Christians must pass their time here in gloom. All is not unpleasant in life. Life is wonderful for those who dare to believe God, and not all the blessings of the Christian life are for the future. Many of us make a grave mistake by not making the best of the opportunities given to us here—because we are always looking to some future event as paramount in our lives.

All of that does not change the fact that each of us will have some heart-wrenching and, at times, overpowering experiences in this life. Life isn't always fair. Sometimes it is unpleasant. Sometimes it is downright depressing. God permits many of the unpleasant experiences of our lives. He has a reason for doing that. He knows what He is doing. He knows what He is working out in our lives. But we don't have to face life's trials alone. He is always with us. How wonderful it is to see His radiant FACE in the hour of our greatest trial!

God did not intend for life's circumstances to embitter us or to cause us to live in constant negativeness and despair. Some of our problems are our own fault. They are the result of our stubbornness or poor choices. We can learn from them. And God will grant us His peace and joy in the midst of any storm. When we see His FACE, we are no longer afraid.

Seeing the FACE of God is a theological controversy, an apparent contradiction. God said to Moses:

You cannot see my FACE, for no one may see me and live."

Exodus 33:20

Jesus said:

No one has ever seen God....

John 1:18

You have never heard his voice nor seen his form.

John 5:37

Paul said:

He is the image of the invisible God, the firstborn over all creation.

Colossians 1:15

Now to the King eternal, immortal, invisible, the only God, be honor and glory for ever and ever. Amen.

1 Timothy 1:17

Whom no one has seen or can see.

1 Timothy 6:16

There is a good reason why God has chosen to remain "*invisible,*" to keep the exact image of His FACE secret to men. If God could be readily seen by man, we would have His pictures plastered everywhere. Endless images would be crafted for His worship and honor, an activity which He has prohibited. He doesn't want us to worship images of Him. He wants us to worship Him.

Still certain Bible characters did see the FACE of God, and reputable believers of every generation have seen Him. What does the Bible mean when it speaks of the FACE of God?

The Hebrew word for FACE is *panim*. It means *countenance* or *disposition, the indexing of the inward thoughts* and *feelings, the presence or the fashion of a company, a visibility, not of the physical features but of ONE which declares or confirms the TRUTH.*

When the Bible speaks of the FACE of God it refers to an expression of God that should settle all fears, erase all doubts, confirm all His greatness, beckon to our affections, and secure and stabilize our relationship with Almighty God. (6)

Adoniram Judson is generally recognized as one of the greatest missionaries of all times. His exploits fill many books. He was a man of deep devotion and dedication to the cause of Christ. This story is told of him:

> "Many years ago, when the great missionary...was home on furlough, he passed through the city of Stonington, Connecticut. A young boy playing about the wharves at the time of Judson's arrival

was struck by the man's appearance. Never before had he seen such a light on any human face. He ran up the street to a minister to ask if he knew who the stranger was. The minister hurried back with him, but became so absorbed in conversation with Judson that he forgot all about the impatient youngster standing near him.

"Many years afterward that boy—who could never get away from the influence of that wonderful face—became the famous preacher Henry Clay Trumbull. In a book of memoirs he penned a chapter entitled: *'What a Boy Saw In The FACE of Adoniram Judson."* That lighted countenance had changed his life." (7)

What the boy saw was not memorable facial features. Rather he sensed the presence of a Holy Company, a visibility declaring something truthful. That FACE spoke to him of compassion and stimulated him to a closer relationship with the Almighty God.

When we consider the FACE of God, we are not considering physical features. We are talking about how His countenance changes us. By design, He has made it impossible to know exactly what He looks like physically. But it is possible for us to be totally changed by a glimpse of His wonderful countenance.

At a future time, we will see God's glory to a greater degree. We will know Him in a more intimate sense.

"And the glory of the Lord will be revealed, and all mankind together will see it. For the mouth of the Lord has spoken."

Isaiah 40:5

But here and now we can know the radiant FACE of our living God; and, when we do, our lives will be changed, as was the life of Jacob.

Until the day that he saw the FACE of God, I find very few good things to say about Jacob as a person. He was the second child born to Isaac and Rebecca. He and Esau were twins, but Jacob was born last. When Rebecca noticed that her pregnancy was not normal, she asked the Lord about it. He told her:

"Two nations are in your womb, and two peoples from within you will be separated; one people will be stronger than the other, and the older will serve the younger."

Genesis 25:23

As the boys grew up, Esau was a hunter and an outdoorsman. However, because she remembered the prophecy over her sons, Rebecca spoiled Jacob. He became a "mama's boy" and didn't wander very far from the house.

The boys grew up, and Esau became a skillful hunter, a man of the open country, while Jacob was a quiet man, staying among the tents."

Genesis 25:27

Isaac loved his eldest, but Rebecca favored the younger son.

> *Isaac, who had a taste for wild game, loved Esau, but Rebekah loved Jacob.*
>
> Genesis 25:28

When it came time for Isaac to pass on the blessing to his eldest son, Rebecca suggested that Jacob deceive his father into thinking that he was Esau and thus gain the blessing for himself. Jacob did not find this deceit unacceptable. He had already learned deceit, and his conscience was dulled to it.

> *Once when Jacob was cooking some stew, Esau came in from the open country, famished. He said to Jacob, "Quick, let me have some of that red stew! I'm famished!" (That is why he was also called Edom.)*
> *Jacob replied, "First sell me your birthright."*
> *"Look, I am about to die," Esau said. "What good is the birthright to me?"*
> *But Jacob said, "Swear to me first." So he swore an oath to him, selling his birthright to Jacob.*
> *Then Jacob gave Esau some bread and some lentil stew. He ate and drank, and then got up and left. So Esau despised his birthright.*
>
> Genesis 25:29-34

Since Esau was the hunter in the family, apparently he had brought the game from which the stew was made. Yet Jacob used it against him in a moment of weakness. Having thus deceived and taken advantage of his brother, it was not a difficult thing for Jacob to accept Rebecca's suggestions of disrespect and deceit toward his father.

> *When Isaac was old and his eyes were so weak that he could no longer see, he called for Esau his older son and said to him, "My son."*
> *"Here I am," he answered.*
> *Isaac said, "I am now an old man and don't know the day of my death. Now then, get your weapons—your quiver and bow—and go out to the open country to hunt some wild game for me. Prepare me the kind of tasty food I like and bring it to me to eat, so that I may give you my blessing before I die."*
>
> Genesis 27:1-4

Sensing that his days were numbered, Isaac requested venison for one of his last meals. Rebecca overheard this conversation. When Esau went out to hunt the meat, she saw her opportunity and convinced Jacob to move quickly.

She told him to get a goat from his father's flock and she would prepare it just the way his father liked it so that he would think it was venison. Jacob eagerly obeyed.

Then she took the skin from the goat and wrapped it over Jacob's hands and neck and she dressed him in Esau's clothes. The idea was that his nearly-blind father would touch him and think that he was indeed Esau. What kind of a brother would do a thing like that? Yet Jacob obeyed.

He went to his father and said, "My father."
"Yes, my son," he answered. "Who is it?"
Jacob said to his father, "I am Esau your firstborn. I have done as you told me. Please sit up and eat some of my game so that you may give me your blessing."
Isaac asked his son, "How did you find it so quickly, my son?"
"The Lord your God gave me success," he replied.
Then Isaac said to Jacob, "Come near so I can touch you, my son, to know whether you really are my son Esau or not." Jacob went close to his father Isaac, who touched him and said, "The voice is the voice of Jacob, but the hands are the hands of Esau." He did not recognize him, for his hands were hairy like those of his brother Esau; so he blessed him. "Are you really my son Esau?" he asked. "I am," he replied.
Then he said, "My son, bring me some of your game to eat, so that I may give you my blessing." Jacob brought it to him and he ate; and he brought some wine and he drank. Then his father Isaac said to him, "Come here, my son, and kiss me." So he went to him and kissed him. When Isaac caught the smell of his clothes, he blessed him and said, "Ah, the smell of my son is like the smell of a field that the Lord has blessed."

Genesis 27:18-27

The deception worked, and Jacob received his father's full blessing. He now had the birthright and the blessing—both through deceit.

Jacob was a coward of sorts and decided to flee rather than face his brother's wrath. By the time Esau had determined to take revenge, Jacob was gone, on his way to the house of his Uncle Laban. During this flight, Jacob had his first encounter with God. He was not really seeking God, but God was seeking him.

> *When he reached a certain place, he stopped for the night because the sun had set. Taking one of the stones there, he put it under his head and lay down to sleep. He had a dream in which he saw a stairway resting on the earth, with its top reaching to heaven, and the angels of God were ascending and descending on it. There above it stood the Lord, and he said: "I am the Lord, the God of your father Abraham and the God of Isaac. I will give you and your descendants the land on which you are lying. Your descendants will be like the dust of the earth, and you will spread out to the west and to the east, to the north and to the south. All peoples on earth will be blessed through you and your offspring. I am with you and will watch over you wherever you go, and I will bring you back to this land. I will not leave you until I have done what I have promised you."*
>
> *When Jacob awoke from his sleep, he thought, "Surely the Lord is in this place, and I was not aware of it." He was afraid and said, "How awesome is this place! This is none other than the house of God; this is the gate of heaven."*
>
> *Early the next morning Jacob took the stone he had placed under his head and set it up as a pillar and*

poured oil on top of it. He called that place Bethel, though the city used to be called Luz.
Then Jacob made a vow, saying, "If God will be with me and will watch over me on this journey I am taking and will give me food to eat and clothes to wear so that I return safely to my father's house, then the Lord will be my God and this stone that I have set up as a pillar will be God's house, and of all that you give me I will give you a tenth."

Genesis 28:11-22

Even after he had such a powerful encounter with the presence of God, Jacob could do no more than make a bargain with his Creator. Some twenty years later he would remember those words.

In the meantime, he went on to his Uncle Laban's house and there fell in love with his cousin Rachel. Laban agreed for Jacob to marry the girl, but only if he worked seven years for her. Because he loved Rachel, Jacob complied.

At the end of the seven years, Laban deceived his nephew and gave him Rachel's older sister Leah. It seems that it wasn't in keeping with the local customs for the younger daughter to marry first. Isn't it interesting that we often are paid with the same currency that we have given out! Deceit breeds deceit.

"If you really want Rachel," Laban told him, "you will have to work another seven years." He did love her, so he consented.

After many years (and ten sons later), Jacob decided to part company with Laban and return to his own home. It was a tense moment.

After Rachel gave birth to Joseph, Jacob said to Laban, "Send me on my way so I can go back to my own homeland. Give me my wives and children, for whom I have served you, and I will be on my way. You know how much work I've done for you."

Genesis 30:25-26

Laban was not happy with the thought of losing Jacob, his two daughters, and his grandchildren. He tried to convince Jacob to stay. But Jacob perpetrated a hoax on his father-in-law to rob him of many of his animals and, because of Laban's anger, was eventually forced to move on. Some people make a mess of everything they do.

When Laban finally released Jacob, he set off with his wives and sons and flocks—and an abiding fear of what it would be like to meet the brother he had defrauded. And, indeed, Esau was looking for a showdown. Jacob knew that he could not run and hide forever, and wondered how to make amends with Esau.

When Jacob's caravan was nearing Edom, the home of his brother, he sent out emissaries to meet and talk with Esau. What they said when they returned terrified him:

Jacob sent messengers ahead of him to his brother Esau in the land of Seir, the country of Edom. He instructed them: "This is what you are to say to my master Esau: 'Your servant Jacob says, I have been staying with Laban and have remained there till now. I have cattle and donkeys, sheep and goats, menservants and maidservants. Now I am sending this message to my lord, that I may find favor in your eyes.'" When the messengers returned to Jacob, they said, "We went to your brother Esau, and now he is coming to meet you, and four hundred men are with him." In great fear and distress Jacob divided the people who were with him into two groups, and the flocks and herds and camels as well.

Genesis 32:3-7

Jacob divided his people into two groups that traveled separately. If Esau came against one group and killed them, at least some of his family would survive.

It was in this moment of crisis that Jacob again turned to God. His once proud, boastful, and deceptive nature was beginning to mellow. He needed God's help. He remembered what God had promised him, and he began to pray.

Then Jacob prayed, "O God of my father Abraham, God of my father Isaac, O Lord, who said to me, 'Go back to your country and your relatives, and I will make you prosper,' I am unworthy of all the kindness and faithfulness you have shown your servant. I had only my staff when I crossed this Jordan, but now I have become two groups. Save me, I pray, from the

> *hand of my brother Esau, for I am afraid he will come and attack me, and also the mothers with their children. But you have said, 'I will surely make you prosper and will make your descendants like the sand of the sea, which cannot be counted.'"*
>
> Genesis 32:9-12

Jacob prepared a very fine gift for his brother (*"two hundred female goats and twenty male goats, two hundred ewes and twenty rams, thirty female camels with their young, forty cows and ten bulls, and twenty female donkeys and ten male donkeys"* [Verses 14-15]) and sent some servants to bring them on their way, hoping to appease Esau's anger.

That night was one Jacob would never forget. While he slept, an angel of the Lord came to him and began to wrestle with him. The two wrestled throughout the night. When the morning had come, the angel perceived that he had not prevailed against Jacob, so he stuck him a blow to the hip that crippled him. When Jacob still would not let go, the stranger begged him: *"Let me go, for it is daybreak"* (Genesis 32:26).

But Jacob replied, *"I will not let you go unless you bless me"* (same verse).

That night Jacob decided, once and for all, that God was the only thing that mattered in his life. All of his possessions suddenly lost their value and sentiment. He had his hands on God. (Bible students agree that although this person who appeared to Jacob is called a "*man,*" there is little doubt that it was an appearance of God Himself, a theophany.) Jacob had his hands on God, and he was determined not to let go. The Lord responded to this change in Jacob's demeanor.

The man asked him, "What is your name?"
"Jacob," he answered.
Then the man said, "Your name will no longer be Jacob, but Israel, because you have struggled with God and with men and have overcome."
Jacob said, "Please tell me your name."
But he replied, "Why do you ask my name?" Then he blessed him there.

Genesis 32:27-29

Jacob's name was changed from that day on, and he renamed the place where he had met God.

So Jacob called the place Peniel, saying, "It is because I saw God FACE to FACE, and yet my life was spared."

Genesis 32:30

Did Jacob actually see the FACE of God? No! But he saw an expression of God that he had never seen before. When he made up his mind that nothing was more dear to him than God and God's will for his life, God gave him an index of his inward feelings and thoughts. God declared himself before Jacob that He was the truth. God settled all of Jacob's fears. God, at that moment, erased all of Jacob's fears. God confirmed His greatness to Jacob. God called for Jacob's affections and devotions. God secured and stabilized his relationship with Jacob, and he was never the same again. God even changed his name to Israel.

Jacob (*ya' aq ob*) means *supplanter, one who uproots and replaces.* That definition had characterized Jacob's life to this point. He had caused constant turmoil to his immediate family with his deception and trickery. After he was married, his wives and sons suffered the consequences of his deceptiveness. But when he came FACE to FACE with God, God changed all of that.

Have you longed for an experience with God that will convince you of His reality and of His truthfulness? Have you longed for an experience that will settle all your fears? Have you longed for God to settle all your doubts? Have you longed for God to confirm to you His greatness? Have you longed for God to call to your affections and devotion? Have you longed for Him to secure and stabilize your relationship with Him and then with everyone else? It can happen when you determine, like Jacob, that you are going to come FACE to FACE with God.

Jacob wasn't the only person who came FACE to FACE with God. There are other examples in the Bible. Moses and David also talked with God FACE to FACE.

The FACE of the Lord became a benediction for Israel.

> *The Lord make his FACE shine upon you and be gracious to you;*
>
> Numbers 6:25

The FACE of the Lord set Israel apart from other nations.

And they will tell the inhabitants of this land about it. They have already heard that you, O Lord, are with these people and that you, O Lord, have been seen FACE to FACE, that your cloud stays over them, and that you go before them in a pillar of cloud by day and a pillar of fire by night.

Numbers 14:14

The FACE of the Lord confirmed the greatness of Moses.

Since then, no prophet has risen in Israel like Moses, whom the Lord knew FACE to FACE,

Deuteronomy 34:10

The FACE of the Lord was what David sought when he was in deep despair.

How long, O Lord? Will you forget me forever? How long will you hide your FACE from me?

Psalms 13:1

The FACE of the Lord was David's ultimate desire.

And I—in righteousness I will see your FACE; when I awake, I will be satisfied with seeing your likeness.

Psalms 17:15

To seek the FACE of the Lord is the commitment of every obedient heart.

My heart says of you, "Seek his FACE!" Your FACE, Lord, I will seek.

Psalms 27:8

Sitting before the FACE of the Lord is the hope of every true believer.

And as for me, thou upholdest me in mine integrity, and settest me before thy FACE for ever.

Psalms 41:12 (KJV)

The FACE of the Lord is the noble cry of the penitent.

May God be gracious to us and bless us and make his FACE shine upon us, Selah .

Psalms 67:1

Hide your FACE from my sins and blot out all my iniquity.

Psalms 51:9

Seeking the FACE of the Lord is a sure step towards restoration.

Restore us, O God; make your FACE shine upon us, that we may be saved.

Psalms 80:3, 19

The Scriptures admonish us to seek God's FACE constantly.

Look to the Lord and his strength; seek his FACE always.

Psalms 105:4

The reason we need to seek the FACE of God is explained to us by the prophet Isaiah.

But your iniquities have separated you from your God; your sins have hidden his FACE from you, so that he will not hear.

Isaiah 59:2

I trust that the knowledge of God's FACE will cause you to seek Him as never before. When you see Him FACE to FACE, it will be a life changing experience, one that you have always longed for. Why not make a determination right now to seek Him as never before. And may the God of Jacob and Moses and David reveal His FACE to you.

Chapter 4

His Convincing MOUTH

For this is what the Lord says—
he who created the heavens, he is God;
he who fashioned and made the earth,

he founded it;
he did not create it to be empty,
but formed it to be inhabited—
he says: "I am the Lord, and there is no other.
I have not spoken in secret,
from somewhere in a land of darkness;
I have not said to Jacob's descendants,
'Seek me in vain.' I, the Lord, SPEAK the truth;
I declare what is right.

"Gather together and come;
assemble, you fugitives from the nations.
Ignorant are those who carry about idols of wood,
who pray to gods that cannot save.
Declare what is to be, present it—

let them take counsel together.
Who foretold this long ago,
who declared it from the distant past?
Was it not I, the Lord?
And there is no God apart from me,
a righteous God and a Savior;
there is none but me.

"Turn to me and be saved, all you ends of the earth;
for I am God, and there is no other.
By myself I have sworn,
my MOUTH has uttered in all integrity
a word that will not be revoked:
Before me every knee will bow;
by me every tongue will swear.
They will say of me, 'In the Lord alone are righteousness and strength.'"
All who have raged against him
will come to him and be put to shame.
But in the Lord all the descendants of Israel
will be found righteous and will exult.

Isaiah 45:18-25

Does God have a MOUTH? Absolutely! And He is still SPEAKING to His people today. While many of us are listening to and relying upon man's weak and faltering answers to the questions of life, God, the Eternal Father, is trying to SPEAK to us through His inspired Word and by the Holy Spirit, whom He has sent to be our Guide into the ways of peace and truth.

There is not nearly enough emphasis in our churches on this wonderful truth.

The Hebrew word for MOUTH is *peh.* It means *an opening, an evidence, and a source for utterance.* (8) Since the meaning is varied, this little word is also used in various ways in the Bible.

Genesis 4:11 speaks of the earth opening *"her MOUTH"* to receive the blood of Abel.

Psalms 141:7 speaks of the *"MOUTH"* of a grave [the door of a tomb], and Joshua 10:18 speaks of the *"MOUTH"* of a cave. [Many graves were actually caves in the side of the rock.]

Genesis 29:2 speaks of the *"MOUTH"* of a well [the opening], and Genesis 42:27 speaks of the *"MOUTH"* [opening] of a bag. Exodus 28:32 describes the opening in a tunic or shirt as its *"MOUTH."*

Isaiah 19:7 speaks of the *"MOUTH"* of a river [where it opens up into the sea].

Proverbs 8:3 describes the entrance into a city as *"the MOUTH."*

So, one meaning of the *MOUTH* of the Lord is the opening to the heart of God. Jesus taught this.

> *But the things that come out of the MOUTH come from the heart....*
>
> Matthew 15:18

The things that proceed out of the MOUTH, come from the heart.

NASV

What comes out of the MOUTH of God shows us what is in His heart. When God SPEAKS, He reveals His heart. God is still SPEAKING to His people, still revealing His heart—in the closing years of the twentieth century.

Because God's Word comes forth from His heart, it cannot be challenged. It is of the highest authority. It is from the purest Source. It is just, complete and final. It is the expression of God's heart.

In the past, there have been essentially six ways in which the MOUTH of GOD has SPOKEN.

The MOUTH of the Lord SPOKE through verbal expression before the Divine inspiration of the written Word.

Immediately after God set in order all the things of creation, He sought to make personal contact with the prize of His creation, man. Of all the elective processes through which He could do so, He chose to do it with His MOUTH.

Even after the fall, God continued to pursue His personal relationship with man, by SPEAKING and revealing His heart.

Then the man and his wife heard the sound of the Lord God as he was walking in the garden in the cool of the day, and they hid from the Lord God among the trees of the garden. But the Lord God called to the man, "Where are you?"

Genesis 3:8-9

The MOUTH of God spoke what the compassionate heart of God felt. God was just as hurt over the transgression of man as was Adam himself. Adam's guilt caused him to want to hide; but God's MOUTH became an instrument of reconciliation.

But now, this is what the Lord says—he who created you, O Jacob, he who formed you, O Israel: "Fear not, for I have redeemed you; I have summoned you by name; you are mine."

Isaiah 43:1

By calling out to them, God was opening up the way for Adam and Eve to experience His heart.

At the baptism of Jesus, an unusual thing happened. The VOICE of God was heard audibly from Heaven.

And the Holy Spirit descended on him in bodily form like a dove. And a voice came from heaven: "You are my Son, whom I love; with you I am well pleased."

Luke 3:22

Hearing the VOICE of God directly from Heaven was the ultimate confirmation of Christ's greatness and authority. No man spoke these words. They came from the heart of God alone.

Intellectual men may have argued about the veracity of the virgin birth, but when many people heard this utterance from Heaven, no one dared question what God had said.

When Jesus was on the Mount of Transfiguration with Peter, James and John, again something unusual happened.

> *While he was still speaking, a bright cloud enveloped them, and a voice from the cloud said, "This is my Son, whom I love; with him I am well pleased. Listen to him!"*
>
> Matthew 17:5

"Listen to Him" is the still most sound advice we can follow these days. All of His words are still valid. All of His truth is still pure. Following His teachings will still bring us into Light. His MOUTH spoke all the heart of God.

The MOUTH of the Lord has always SPOKEN through nature.

> *The heavens declare the glory of God;*
> *the skies proclaim the work of his hands.*
> *Day after day they pour forth speech;*
> *night after night they display knowledge.*
> *There is no speech or language*
> *where their voice is not heard.*
>
> Psalms 19:1-3

Because God SPEAKS through the many wonderful things of creation, no one is left with an excuse not to know Him. Through nature He SPEAKS in such a way that no culture nor language inhibits understanding.

The MOUTH of the Lord SPOKE through the ancient prophets.

> *In the past God spoke to our forefathers through the prophets at many times and in various ways.*
>
> Hebrews 1:1

> *For prophecy never came by the will of man, but holy men of God spoke as they were moved by the Holy Spirit.*
>
> 2 Peter 1:21 (NKJV)

In each generation, God used men whom He could trust to be His MOUTHPIECE and declare His will. The ultimate goal of every pastor, every teacher, every evangelist, every missionary, every Sunday school worker, and every witness should be to convey to others the very heart of GOD. In the degree that we do this, we become the instruments of God's MOUTH to our generations.

The MOUTH of the Lord SPOKE through the person of Jesus of Nazareth, the Christ.

> *But in these last days he has SPOKEN to us by his Son, whom he appointed heir of all things, and through whom he made the universe. The Son is the radiance of God's glory and the exact representation of his being, sustaining all things by his powerful word.*

After he had provided purification for sins, he sat down at the right hand of the Majesty in heaven.

Hebrews 1:2-3

The MOUTH of the Lord SPOKE (and continues to SPEAK) through the Holy Spirit.

Nehemiah gave credit to the Spirit for his ability to SPEAK the heart of God.

You gave your good Spirit to instruct them. You did not withhold your manna from their mouths, and you gave them water for their thirst.

Nehemiah 9:20

When Jesus had finished His earthly ministry and was about to return to Heaven, He said:

But the Counselor, the Holy Spirit, whom the Father will send in my name, will teach you all things and will remind you of everything I have said to you.

John 14:26

Many of the words of Jesus were later written down and became part of what we now recognize as the written Word of God. But Jesus credited the Holy Spirit with teaching us all things [causing us to understand the words of Jesus] and reminding us of everything that Jesus had said. These are two of the most powerful and fruitful of the Holy Spirit's many works.

Nothing could be more important in our lives than the Word of God. If we take time to read it and study it, the Spirit has something with which to work. In order to know God's heart we must be saturating our minds with His Word.

The MOUTH of the Lord SPEAKS through His Word.

God's written Word has become the standard of measurement for every other expression. His Word is pure and perfect and gives us clear entrance into His Heart. It enables us to understand His authority.

God set the precedence for His Word in the Old Testament by giving the law to His people. Through Moses, God established that He would nourish His people [feed them from the goodness of His heart] through the Word.

> *Remember how the Lord your God led you all the way in the desert these forty years, to humble you and to test you in order to know what was in your heart, whether or not you would keep his commands. He humbled you, causing you to hunger and then feeding you with manna, which neither you nor your fathers had known, to teach you that man does not live on bread alone but on every word that comes from the MOUTH of the Lord.*
>
> Deuteronomy 8:2-3

These days everyone is concerned about the proper diet, about eating the proper foods in order to have good health. How much more important our spiritual diet is! Feeding regularly on the Word of God means the difference between life and death.

God's MOUTH SPEAKS peace:

I will take away the chariots from Ephraim and the war-horses from Jerusalem, and the battle bow will be broken. He will proclaim peace to the nations. His rule will extend from sea to sea and from the River to the ends of the earth.

Zechariah 9:10

God's MOUTH SPEAKS prosperity to the obedient:

Every man will sit under his own vine and under his own fig tree, and no one will make them afraid, for the Lord Almighty has spoken.

Micah 4:4

But if you resist and rebel, you will be devoured by the sword." For the MOUTH of the Lord has spoken.

Isaiah 1:20

God's MOUTH SPEAKS newness to our lives:

The nations will see your righteousness, and all kings your glory; you will be called by a new name that the MOUTH of the Lord will bestow.

Isaiah 62:2

No longer will they call you Deserted, or name your land Desolate. But you will be called Hephzibah, and your land Beulah; for the Lord will take delight in you, and your land will be married.

Isaiah 62:4

To them I will give within my temple and its walls a memorial and a name better than sons and daughters; I will give them an everlasting name that will not be cut off.

Isaiah 56:5

Nothing is worse than having developed a bad name. Such a stigma often sticks with a person for life. Long after the public forgets the rumors and pays no more attention to the scandals, the bitterness of having spoiled one's name still lingers in the mind of the individual affected. It is like a plague.

Years after I had graduated from high school, I met a couple in church. The wife turned out to be a former classmate of mine. I had forgotten her maiden name, so I asked. I will never forget her response: "I would rather not tell you. I had a very bad name then."

So many people are ashamed of their past and would like to just change their name altogether. God says He can do that. He can remove all the guilt and SPEAK newness to our lives.

The MOUTH of the Lord SPEAKS assurance.

Then you will find your joy in the Lord, and I will cause you to ride on the heights of the land and to feast on the inheritance of your father Jacob." The MOUTH of the Lord has spoken.

Isaiah 58:14

The MOUTH of the Lord SPEAKS openly.

I have not SPOKEN in secret, in a dark place of the earth: I said not unto the seed of Jacob, Seek ye me in vain: I the Lord SPEAK righteousness, I declare things that are right.

Isaiah 45:19 (KJV)

I am so amused with the "secret" conversations of teenagers. When they get a special phone call, they move off into a corner somewhere; their voices become subdued; and they carry on some "top secret" conversation. When they are finished with all the "secrets," they move back into range and raise their voices to normal levels before hanging up. I wish they could see themselves. They are so obvious.

God doesn't have any secrets. He doesn't SPEAK in hushed tones in dark places.

Some of the "*secret*" conversations of teenagers are about personal and sensitive matters. That is why they make efforts to guard in secrecy what they say. God always speaks "*righteousness*" and openly declares "*things that are right.*"

He is calling us to hear His VOICE today.

"Gather together and come; assemble, you fugitives from the nations. Ignorant are those who carry about idols of wood, who pray to gods that cannot save. Declare what is to be, present it—let them take counsel together. Who foretold this long ago, who declared

it from the distant past? Was it not I, the Lord? And there is no God apart from me, a righteous God and a Savior; there is none but me.

Isaiah 45:20-21

Hearing what God SPEAKS demands a change in our way of life. We must abandon our ways and accept His better ways. Why not? His ways lead to peace now and life everlasting.

Someone has said that the reason God created man with two ears and just one MOUTH is that He wants us to listen twice as much as we SPEAK. There is a lot of truth in that.

Many of us wish that we could hear God's voice, but we simply haven't known how. Jesus told us how to hear from the heavenly Father.

But when you pray, go into your room, close the door and pray to your Father, who is unseen. Then your Father, who sees what is done in secret, will reward you.

Matthew 6:6

Hearing from the MOUTH of God requires that we remove ourselves from other distractions, from the other voices around us that seek to influence us. We must take the initiative to get alone with God and thus give Him the opportunity to SPEAK.

Very much as a lover, He desires times of privacy and intimacy in which He can express to us the deepest desires of His heart.

Do you know my Father in this way? If you are willing to take the necessary time to get to know Him, you will never be sorry. He will turn your life around completely.

His is a very personal MOUTH.

One of the most frustrating experiences of our time is our increased reliance on the answering machine. When we try to reach someone by telephone, we get either a busy signal or a recording.

A busy signal tells us that the person that we want to talk to is talking to someone else. That precludes a conversation with us—at the moment.

The answering machine is even worse. What we hear is not a living person but a synthetic reproduction, a recording, and the message is old. The voice isn't alive or active.

I know that answering machines have their advantages, and that is why we are using them more and more. But I also know what a disappointment it is to get a recording when we need a real person.

Thank God that His MOUTH is never too busy. He can be talking to millions of others at the same moment, yet He always has time for me. The message that proceeds from His MOUTH is never old. It is always current, even prophetic. Let God SPEAK to you today.

Chapter 5

His Incomparable MIND

Do you not know? Have you not heard? The Lord is the everlasting God, the Creator of the ends of the earth. He will not grow tired or weary, and his understanding no one can fathom.

Isaiah 40:28

"Who has known the MIND of the Lord? Or who has been his counselor?"

Romans 11:34

For who has known the MIND of the Lord that he may instruct him?"

1 Corinthians 2:16

Needless to say the MIND that set in order the whole of creation is a vast subject, one that none of us will ever fully comprehend.

The Human MIND

Even the human MIND, which God designed, is an amazing thing. No computer built to date can come close to matching it. We are told that the average person has ten thousand thoughts a day or more than 3.5 million thoughts a year. And there are many people living who could in no way be considered average. They are geniuses.

One of the most remarkable people I have ever heard of was Henry Blinn, and elder of the Shaker community in Canterbury, New Hampshire. He lived from 1824 to 1905. As was the modest custom of the Shakers, Henry was celibate. He never married; and he fathered no children.

The Shakers only multiplied by adoption. They took in homeless and orphaned children willing to take the vows of their faith and be governed completely by their religious and moral tenets.

The community was dedicated to the education of all their children, their vocational training and their integration into useful society. When a youngster came to the Shakers, they would first attempt to discover his strengths. Over a period of a month, skilled elders, who were willing to donate their time and had the patience to work with children, first taught a series of vocational crafts. They included: herdsmanship, carpentry, tinsmithing, blacksmithing, farming, maple sugaring and fence building—all very practical skills for their time.

During this time they were able to determine where this particular child's strengths lay and could begin the formal training for his vocation within the Shaker community. Henry Blinn was one of the most famous of these elders, famous only in his immediate community.

What a MIND he had! Although he had no formal education at all, he was a self-taught chemist. He developed a paint that has lasted over a hundred years. Some of the original luster has vanished, but little or none of the color. Because the Shakers didn't believe in patenting anything, no records were kept of the paint's contents. Several leading paint manufacturers have taken sample paint chips in an effort to discover Henry's secret.

He was a precision cabinet maker. A master at dove-tailing and mortise work, his creations included the manufacturing of the famous Shaker furniture. His work in wood has been widely copied but never equaled.

He was a self-taught dentist. He performed all the dental work for the residents of the commune, as well as for many of the surrounding neighbors. They trusted his work.

He was also a barber.

Henry Blinn took no credit for his work. He gave all the credit to God. He said that God taught him everything he knew.

People like Henry Blinn challenge us to the fact that we are tapping only a small measure of the ability God has given each of us.

The MIND receives signals from certain nerve centers of our body and allows us to respond to pain, heat, and cold. The MIND controls all the emotions and all the movements of the body in response to those emotions.

In essence, the MIND processes everything received from the body and emotions and begins to program some sort of action or reaction. It receives information from the eyes and identifies what is being seen. It receives the sound processed through the ear and identifies what is being heard—whether pleasant and peaceful or loud and alarming. It receives what comes through the nose and identifies what is being smelled. It receives what comes through the taste buds and decides if it is something that is pleasing to the palate or not.

It is the MIND which ultimately decides what to do with the information it receives. And how the person reacts is the result of how the MIND has processed the information it has received.

In this regard, the Christian has every advantage; for there is a degenerate MIND and there is a regenerated MIND. When Adam and Even fell into sin and disobedience, they lost much of the potential with which the MIND was originally designed. Sin dulls the MIND. A MIND that rejects the realities of Christ is clearly defined in the Scriptures.

The unregenerate MIND is vain (idle).

Do not let anyone who delights in false humility and the worship of angels disqualify you for the prize.

Such a person goes into great detail about what he has seen, and his unspiritual MIND puffs him up with idle notions.

Colossians 2:18

Let no man beguile you of your reward in a voluntary humility and worshipping of angels, intruding into those things which he hath not seen, vainly puffed up by his fleshly MIND,

Colossians 2:18 (KJV)

The unregenerate MIND is carnal (sinful).

Because the carnal MIND is enmity against God: for it is not subject to the law of God, neither indeed can be.

Romans 8:7 (KJV)

The sinful MIND is hostile to God. It does not submit to God's law, nor can it do so.

Romans 8:7

The unregenerate MIND is reprobate (degenerate).

Furthermore, since they did not think it worthwhile to retain the knowledge of God, he gave them over to a depraved MIND, to do what ought not to be done.

Romans 1:28

And even as they did not like to retain God in their knowledge, God gave them over to a reprobate MIND, to do those things which are not convenient.

Romans 1:28 (KJV)

The unregenerate MIND is defiled (corrupted).

Unto the pure all things are pure: but unto them that are defiled and unbelieving is nothing pure; but even their MIND and conscience is defiled.

Titus 1:15 (KJV)

To the pure, all things are pure, but to those who are corrupted and do not believe, nothing is pure. In fact, both their minds and consciences are corrupted.

Titus 1:15

The MIND of a person who has accepted Christ and His truth begins a process of renovation. It is also clearly defined in Scripture.

The MIND of a person converted to Christ is renewed.

Do not conform any longer to the pattern of this world, but be transformed by the renewing of your MIND. Then you will be able to test and approve what God's will is—his good, pleasing and perfect will.

Romans 12:2

The MIND of a person converted to Christ is ready.

These were more noble than those in Thessalonica, in that they received the word with all readiness of MIND, and searched the scriptures daily, whether those things were so.

Acts 17:11 (KJV)

The MIND of a person converted to Christ is unified.

> *Fulfil ye my joy, that ye be likeminded, having the same love, being of one accord, of one MIND.*
>
> Philippians 2:2 (KJV)

The MIND of God

The human MIND is geared mainly for survival. God's MIND, on the other hand, is geared to design, to create. He understands all that has ever been and all that ever will be. What a mighty God we serve! No wonder we cannot fully comprehend the greatness of His MIND!

The MIND of God is designed to govern the affairs of mankind.

The first reference to the MIND of GOD is found in Leviticus.

> *And they put him in ward, that the MIND of the Lord might be shewed them.*
>
> Leviticus 24:12 (KJV)

Two young boys got into a fight, probably racially motivated. One of them was Jewish, while the other was mixed, Jewish and Egyptian. During the fight, the Jewish boy cursed [blasphemed] the name of God. Because of the reverence they had for the name of the Lord, the people placed that boy in custody *"until the MIND of the Lord be made clear unto them"* concerning this matter (The Living Bible).

The MIND of the Lord is the will of the Lord. It is that which the Lord has determined will happen.

God's will, first of all, is that He be honored. A violation of that honor carries with it certain consequences for the offender. The consequences, in this particular case were severe.

> *Then the Lord said to Moses: "Take the blasphemer outside the camp. All those who heard him are to lay their hands on his head, and the entire assembly is to stone him. Say to the Israelites: 'If anyone curses his God, he will be held responsible; anyone who blasphemes the name of the Lord must be put to death. The entire assembly must stone him. Whether an alien or native-born, when he blasphemes the Name, he must be put to death.'"*
>
> Leviticus 24:13-16

We might ask ourselves where the mercy of the Lord was on this occasion. The answer can come only as we understand the MIND from which these words emanated. Our finite minds limit us in our understanding of the matter.

Paul enlightens us to the scope of the MIND of the Lord.

> *For God has bound all men over to disobedience so that he may have mercy on them all.*
> *Oh, the depth of the riches of the wisdom and knowledge of God!*
> *How unsearchable his judgments, and his paths*

beyond tracing out!
"Who has known the MIND of the Lord?
Or who has been his counselor?"

Romans 11:32-34

After the fall of Adam and Eve in the Garden, God determined that His greatness would be revealed to man's generations through His MIND, His will. That MIND is so complete and so incomprehensible that no one has ever known it completely. Eternity will hardly be time enough for God to expose His thoughts, His reasoning, and His design.

As our MIND is to our own bodies, God's MIND is to all the universe. As the human MIND receives from the body the different messages and forges a response, the MIND of God receives messages from the body of His creation and programs the needed actions.

As God's eyes run to and from throughout the whole earth, seeking hearts that will respond to Him, His MIND interprets what His eyes see and tells Him when He has spotted such a person.

As His ears are inclined to man's level, and as they sensitively listen to the cry on man's heart, God's MIND interprets what His ears have heard and causes Him to respond to that cry.

As God's face beholds the life that has been to Jabbok and poured out its hurting soul before Him, and has wrestled with God to the point that there has been a Peniel established, a place where God prevails, His

MIND picks up the message and begins to share a greater degree of intimacy with that person.

As God's mouth relates His word to man in one of many ways, God's MIND picks up the signals of who acts in obedience to that word and rushes additional information about Himself that will further cement the relationship.

God's MIND governs creation with intensity.

As we have seen, Isaiah calls our God "*the Creator of the ends of the Earth.*" He had a great insight into His incomparable MIND.

> *Who has measured the waters in the hollow of his hand, or with the breadth of his hand marked off the heavens? Who has held the dust of the earth in a basket, or weighed the mountains on the scales and the hills in a balance?*
>
> Isaiah 40:12

> *Before him all the nations are as nothing.*
>
> Isaiah 40:17

> *He sits enthroned above the circle of the earth, and its people are like grasshoppers. He stretches out the heavens like a canopy, and spreads them out like a tent to live in.*
>
> Isaiah 40:22

It was by reading this verse that Columbus knew the earth was round.

"To whom will you compare me? Or who is my equal?" says the Holy One.

Isaiah 40:25

That's a very good question. Job confronted the same mystery, as did David.

"But he stands alone, and who can oppose him? He does whatever he pleases."

Job 23:13

But the plans of the Lord stand firm forever, the purposes of his heart through all generations.

Psalms 33:11

The MIND of God was ever present in creation. After everything was made, He and He alone could say that it was "*good.*" It had to be good. Everything that He has ever done or ever will do has been done by Divine appointment, in His time, and according to His will.

Everything in creation was obedient to God—except His prized creation, man. Rather than enjoy the goodness which God had created, he chose to rebel against the Almighty and take sides with a loser against Him. When he fell, instead of repenting and returning to the fold of God's favor, he accelerated his evil and forced God to take remedial action.

Isaiah tells us that: God does not faint [He doesn't get tired of us]. He is not weary [or exhausted]. There is no searching of His understanding. [Everything He does is to satisfy Himself. This may not make any sense to us right now, but ultimately we will understand everything.]

God warned the children of Israel about their disobedience.

> *This is what the Lord says: "Go and buy a clay jar from a potter. Take along some of the elders of the people and of the priests and go out to the Valley of Ben Hinnom, near the entrance of the Potsherd Gate. There proclaim the words I tell you, and say, 'Hear the word of the Lord, O kings of Judah and people of Jerusalem. This is what the Lord Almighty, the God of Israel, says: Listen! I am going to bring a disaster on this place that will make the ears of everyone who hears of it tingle. For they have forsaken me and made this a place of foreign gods; they have burned sacrifices in it to gods that neither they nor their fathers nor the kings of Judah ever knew, and they have filled this place with the blood of the innocent. They have built the high places of Baal to burn their sons in the fire as offerings to Baal—something I did not command or mention, nor did it enter my MIND.' "*
>
> Jeremiah 19:1-5

Jeremiah was to take the people into the "Valley of Ben Hinnom" and there tell them that because they had not heeded God's pleas, He would destroy them. God had already established his MIND.

> *This is the word that came to Jeremiah from the Lord: "Go down to the potter's house, and there I will give*

you my message." So I went down to the potter's house, and I saw him working at the wheel. But the pot he was shaping from the clay was marred in his hands; so the potter formed it into another pot, shaping it as seemed best to him.
Then the word of the Lord came to me: "O house of Israel, can I not do with you as this potter does?" declares the Lord. "Like clay in the hand of the potter, so are you in my hand, O house of Israel."

Jeremiah 18:1-6

This is the message of the MIND of God: "Because I don't get tired of you, because you cannot exhaust Me, I am willing to collect the information of your failures, take your life in My hands, break up the damaged parts of your life and reshape you into a most valuable vessel."

What a wonderful God we serve!

Have you ever attempted to create something with your hands, only to run out of patience and become throughly frustrated as a result? Did you feel like throwing your creation into the trash? If so, you know what it is to faint and become weary. Most of us have been there and understand that scenario.

God made man in His own image. Yet man has consistently become marred and scarred and disfigured through his insistence upon sin and rebellion.

Still the MIND of God is to be patient and give us another chance. God is willing to try again with a failed vessel. He is ready to go the second mile. He knows the destiny of that vessel. He knows the glory of His plan for that child. He knows that if a person can get straightened out, they will be valuable—to God, to themselves and to others.

God's MIND is past finding out. He knows the end from the beginning. He has a plan for each of His creatures. He has a positive MIND. He isn't willing to give up on anyone.

God's MIND governs creation with security (assurance).

God never has to second-guess a given situation. Because of our limited understanding or because of our inability to make a proper decision, we second-guess many situations and guess wrongly. God is truth. He knows all. He understands all. He made it all. So, He never has to guess. And He is never wrong.

He is the beginning of all time.
He is the origin of all matter.
He is the plan of all peace.
He is the compass for all directions.
He is the future of all plans.
He is the action to all movement.
He is the food for all thought.
He is the instruction for all teachers.
He is the counsel or all counselors.
He is the health for all sickness.
And who can possibly know His MIND?

This is why Isaiah could say of God:

> *"For my thoughts are not your thoughts, neither are your ways my ways," declares the Lord. "As the heavens are higher than the earth, so are my ways higher than your ways and my thoughts than your thoughts."*
>
> Isaiah 55:8-9

Jeremiah saw into the workings of God's MIND when he said:

> *For I know the thoughts that I think toward you saith the Lord, thoughts of peace, and not of evil, to give you an expected end [a Divinely-appointed end]. Then shall you call upon me, and you shall go and pray unto me, and I will hearken unto you. And you shall seek me, and find me, when you shall search for me with all your heart.*
>
> Jeremiah 29:11-13

With that, the promise of Isaiah makes more sense.

> *Thou wilt keep him in perfect peace, whose MIND is stayed on Thee, because he trusteth in Thee. Trust ye in the Lord forever; for in the Lord God is everlasting strength.*
>
> Isaiah 26:3-4 (KJV)

Do you know Him? If not, make Him your God today.

Chapter 6

His Compassionate HEART

"For God so loved the world that he gave his one and only Son, that whoever believes in him shall not perish but have eternal life."

John 3:16

The Human HEART

The physical HEART is a life-giving pump, a simple machine with a sacred mission. Its labor is brute, its fabric coarse, yet the HEART connects and sustains the body's work. Cardiac rhythm allows the brain to think, the lungs to breathe and the muscles to move. The HEART is the center of life. A seventeenth century doctor, William Harvey, deemed the HEART *"the sovereign of the body."*

The HEART kindles and keeps life's flame. In pregnancy's fourth week, a cluster of cells inside the growing embryo suddenly gains purpose. Inexplicably the cells begin to pulse, sparking a cadence that will continue throughout life. Small wonder that the Greek philosopher Aristotle thought the HEART was the first organ to live and the last organ to die, an organ from which the motions of the body commence.

The great artist, Leonardo da Vinci, a life-long student of anatomy said: *"With what words will you describe the HEART, so as not to fill a book."*

The Egyptians weighed the hearts of the dead to measure truth. The Greeks saw the HEART as a forge, burning impurities from the blood. The ancients thought the HEART to contain the spiritual essence of man and not the physiological.

Today, we know the HEART to be a technical masterpiece. From it springs life, bound to the virtue of honor, love, and courage. The HEART ties the body to spirit, the mystical past to the practical present.

When the Bible speaks of the HEART it usually does not mean the physical pump that circulates the blood. The Hebrew word for HEART is leb, meaning: *the center of feelings, the seat of desires, affections, emotions, and love, the most interior organ of a being.*

The human HEART is sensitive. Solomon in Proverbs declared:

> *A merry HEART maketh a cheerful countenance: but by sorrow of the HEART the spirit is broken.*
>
> 15:13 (KJV)

A happy HEART makes the face cheerful, but heartache crushes the spirit.

15:13

A merry HEART doeth good like a medicine: but a broken spirit drieth the bones.

17:22 (KJV)

A cheerful HEART is good medicine, but a crushed spirit dries up the bones.

17:22

Just by language, hearts can break, they can sing, turn as hard as stone, become heavy, light, cold or warm. Character is determined by the condition of the HEART.

The Chinese physician, Nei Ching, believed: "Putting bad ideas into practice would damage the HEART."

From the HEART flows the deepest issues of life. The feelings and emotions of our being. When our HEART is grieved or broken, it greatly affects our feelings and emotions.

We are told that mankind in America today suffers 4,000 HEART attacks each day. This totals some 1.5 million each year. The number of those who have wounded or broken hearts are at even higher figures. Once the HEART has been damaged, either emotionally or physically, there is a sensitivity about it that seeks to guard and protect against any re-occurrence.

God said of the HEART:

The HEART is deceitful above all things, and desperately wicked: who can know it?

Jeremiah 17:9 (KJV)

The HEART is deceitful above all things and beyond cure. Who can understand it?

Jeremiah 17:9

Since the fall of man, God's assessment of the HEART has proved true.

Dr. Christian Barnard, the South African surgeon who pioneered HEART transplant surgery, taught us a great deal about the HEART—physical and otherwise. Because of his now-famous work in the field of HEART surgery, he was able to write a book for those who suffer from HEART disease. *Heart Attack* helped thousands of such people to better understand the maladies which afflicted them.

His wife wrote a very different type of book about the HEART. After the good doctor left her for a younger and wealthier woman, and after a very bitter divorce proceeding, she wrote a book entitled *HEART Break.* It was directed to women who found themselves rejected by their husbands and offered them hope for some semblance of future. (9)

There is another sense in which the word HEART is used in the Bible and in everyday life. Since the HEART is the most innermost organ of the body, the

HEART is also the most hidden part of anything. Out of the HEART comes the collective energies of a being. The Scriptures mention: the HEART of the sea (Exodus 15:8), the HEART of a tree (2 Samuel 18:14), and the HEART of the earth (Matthew 12:40).

It is in the HEART of man that the moral and spiritual condition is found. Jesus said that the things that defile are not external things but those things that come from within, out of an impure HEART:

> *"For out of the HEART come evil thoughts, murder, adultery, sexual immorality, theft, false testimony, slander. These are what make a man 'unclean'; but eating with unwashed hands does not make him 'unclean.'"*
>
> Matthew 15:19-20

The HEART of God

The HEART of God is so different from the HEART of man. It is a HEART of COMPASSION.

A Jewish legend says: "*When God was about to create man, He took into His counsel the angels that stood about His throne.*

> *"Create him not," said the angel of Justice, "for if Thou dost, he will commit all kinds of wickedness against his fellow man: he will be hard and cruel, dishonest and unrighteous."*
>
> *"Create him not," said the angel of Truth, "for he will be false and deceitful to his brother-man, and even to Thee."*

> *"Create him not," said the angel of Holiness, "he will follow that which is impure in Thy sight, and dishonor Thee to thy face."*
> *Then stepped forward the angel of Mercy (God's best beloved) and said: "Create him, Our Heavenly Father, for when he sins and turns from the path of right and truth and holiness, I will take him tenderly by the hand, and speak loving words to him, and then lead him back to Thee."* (10)

No pit has ever been so deep as the failures of mankind. Only a special HEART of compassion can handle the grief that these failures have caused, as this story illustrates.

"At the age of 32, William Cowper passed through a great crisis in his life. He tried to end his life by taking laudanum [a combination of opium and alcohol]. Then he hired a horse-drawn cabbie, ordering the driver to take him to the Thames, intending to throw himself from the bridge. It was one of London's foggiest nights. They drove for an hour without reaching the chosen spot. Disgusted, he decided to get out and walk there. He found to his surprise they had actually gone in a circle and he was back at his own doorstep.

"The next morning, he fell upon a knife; but the blade broke, and his life was spared. He then tried to hang himself, and was cut down, unconscious, but still alive.

"Then one morning, in a moment of strange cheerfulness, he took up his Bible and read a verse in the letter to the Romans. In a moment he received strength to believe and rejoiced in the forgiving power of God. Sometime later, William Cowper summed up his faith in God's loving dealing with him in a great hymn which became a favorite among Christians:

"God moves in a mysterious way
His wonders to perform:
He plants His footsteps in the sea.
And rides upon the storm.

"Deep in unfathomable mines
Of never failing skill
He treasures up His bright designs,
And works His sovereign will.

"Ye fearful saints, fresh courage take.
The clouds ye so much dread
Are big with mercy, and shall break
In blessings on your head.

"Judge not the Lord by feeble sense,
But trust Him for His grace:
Behind a frowning providence
He hides a smiling face.

"His purposes will ripen fast
Unfolding every hour;
The bud may have a bitter taste
But sweet will be the flower.

"Blind unbelief is sure to err,
And scan His work in vain;
God is His own interpreter
And He will make it plain." (11)

Only God could lift a man from such depth of despair and put such a wonderful song in his HEART. God loves the world. He loves men and women. He loves you and me.

The primary function of the HEART of God is love.

Love is not an emotion but rather a conscious decision made by the mind of a person. God loves because He wants to, and His love has produced the most remarkable statement in Scriptures. He loved us so much that He sent His only Son to die in our place. What a wonderful love! That one verse says it all.

Is there anything in this world worthy of such a commitment on God's part? Is there a person deserving of such an act of God's compassion? He never asked that question. I did. He loved, so He gave.

Nearly half of the population of our world goes to bed hungry every night. That's nearly three billion people. Does anyone care? Yes, God does.

Does He care about what is happening in America? Statistics from 1986 show that Americans were subject to:

20,610	Murders
90,430	Forcible Rapes
542,780	Robberies
834,320	Aggravated Assaults
3,241,400	Burglaries
7,257,200	Thefts (Larceny)
1,224,100	Motor Vehicle thefts

25,000	deaths caused by alcohol
50,000	killed by highway accidents

Not to mention the countless deaths caused by drugs and thousands of other deaths and accidents of *"suspicious origin."*

Does He care? Oh, yes He does! He loves this world. It may be torn by prejudice, strife, economic manipulation, the peril of war, the division over religious preference. It may be plunging down a course toward self-destruction. But He cares. Believe me, He does.

When considering the implications of John 3:16, G. Campbell Morgan, the Great English clergyman and teacher (affectionately referred to as the "Prince of Expositors"), said: *"This is a text that I never attempted to preach on....It is too big. ...If we only knew how to read it, so as to produce a sense of it in the ears of people, there would be nothing to preach about."* (12) He knew what he was talking about, for he said this after fifty years of successful and effective ministry.

This one small verse gives us dimensional insight into the HEART of God:

"The breadth of His love:	'God so loved the world'
"The length of His love:	'That He gave His only begotten Son'
"The depth of His love:	'That whosoever believeth in Him shall not perish'
"The height of His love:	'But shall have everlasting life.'" (13)

Martin Luther, the great transformationist, called John 3:16 *"the HEART of the Bible—the Gospel in miniature." It presents, he said:*

"God	The greatest Lover
"So loved	The greatest degree
"The world	The greatest number
"That He gave	The greatest act
"His only begotten Son	The greatest gift
"That whosoever	The greatest invitation
"Believeth	The greatest simplicity
"In Him	The greatest Person
"Should not perish	The greatest deliverance
"But	The greatest difference
"Have	The greatest certainty
"Everlasting life	THE GREATEST POSSESSION" (14)

Since the HEART is the center of all emotions, affections and desires, the HEART of God reveals to us the purity of His character. The love that flows from God's HEART is the clearest indication of a rational, voluntary action, having its ground in the purest form of truth, holiness, and the exercise of free choice.

We all marvel at the wonders of creation. When we begin to understand the HEART of God we can see the reasoning behind the creation.

In his Epistle to the Ephesians, Paul gives us some wonderful insight into the scope of God's plan.

Praise be to the God and Father of our Lord Jesus Christ, who has blessed us in the heavenly realms with every spiritual blessing in Christ. For he chose us in him before the creation of the world to be holy and blameless in his sight. In love he predestined us to be adopted as his sons through Jesus Christ, in accordance with his pleasure and will—to the praise of his glorious grace, which he has freely given us in the One he loves. In him we have redemption through his blood, the forgiveness of sins, in accordance with the riches of God's grace that he lavished on us with all wisdom and understanding. And he made known to us the mystery of his will according to his good pleasure, which he purposed in Christ, to be put into effect when the times will have reached their fulfillment—to bring all things in heaven and on earth together under one head, even Christ.

In him we were also chosen, having been predestined according to the plan of him who works out everything in conformity with the purpose of his will, in order that we, who were the first to hope in Christ, might be for the praise of his glory. And you also were included in Christ when you heard the word of truth, the gospel of your salvation. Having believed, you were marked in him with a seal, the promised Holy Spirit, who is a deposit guaranteeing our inheritance until the redemption of those who are God's possession—to the praise of his glory.

Ephesians 1:3-14

The Living Bible says in verses 4 and 5:

Long ago, before He made the world, God chose us to be His very own, through what Christ would do for us. His unchanging plan has always been to adopt us into His own family by sending Jesus to die for us. And He did this because HE WANTED TO!

"He wanted to." That is the manifestation of God's love. Deep in the center of His being, at the control center of all His love and affections, His great compassionate HEART:

Planned out a forgiveness before we ever failed.
Developed a relationship with us before we were even formed.
Established a place for us to spend eternity before we even die.
Has set for us an inheritance that we can receive a little of before we get there to help us understand how wonderful it is.

The ultimate function of the HEART of God is to love, and the object of that love is the most contrary of all creatures, man. Still, God's HEART does not harden against man. His love is pure; and pure love knows no degrees. It is limitless.

God's HEART does feel. He wants us to respond to His love, and our response brings Him joy. We "bless" the Lord by reacting positively to His call.

He doesn't expect something of us that we are unable to give. He understands our limitations as humans and promises to help us by giving us a new HEART to replace the HEART that has been infected by transgression and rebellion.

I will give you a new HEART and put a new spirit in you; I will remove from you your HEART of stone and give you a HEART of flesh.

Ezekiel 36:26

What God does to our hearts is very much like the jump starting we occasionally have to do to our batteries. Automotive batteries are wonderful things; but when they get older or worn or during very cold periods, they just can't do what they were designed to do. They cannot properly hold a charge and must be either recharged or replaced. In the meantime, we jump start them from a battery that is good.

Sin has taken all the life out of the human HEART, rendering it powerless to do what it was designed to do. We need a jump start from the HEART of God. We need to get hooked up to His life. We need to be reconnected to His love.

Until that happens, we are "*dead in our transgressions and sins.*"

As for you, you were dead in your transgressions and sins, in which you used to live when you followed the ways of this world and of the ruler of the kingdom of the air, the spirit who is now at work in those who are disobedient.

Ephesians 2:1-2

God sent His only Son, Jesus Christ, to be the heavenly jumper cable, to reconnect God and man and to send a new charge of life into those who were willing to get connected. He gives us a new HEART, a fresh start in life.

God's HEART knows no boundaries; and you and I are a testimony to that fact. He has gone to incredible depths to "jump start" humanity. He does it because He wants to. He does it because He has a HEART of compassion. Making contact with the wrecked and ruined and wasted lives of men and women brings Him great happiness.

God's HEART is accessible.

The human HEART has a tolerance level. When we get our hearts broken or grieved, we develop a barrier that seeks to guard and protect the HEART against any further damage. Feelings are cut off; sensitivity is turned away; and barriers are put up to block further access. We become distant and distrustful of others and build a wall of resentment and bitterness around our lives which keeps others out. We still have the same emotional needs as always, but we satisfy ourselves to live without their fulfillment rather than risk of being hurt again.

The HEART of God has been broken and grieved by the constant rejection of man down through the centuries. Yet, He refuses to build the type of barrier to fellowship that we are prone to erect. Through it all, He remains accessible to man and still invites us to know and share His innermost feeling.

The Levitical priests prayed:

In all that has happened to us, you have been just; you have acted faithfully, while we did wrong.

Nehemiah 9:33

These priests were ordained of God to be His representatives to their fellow man. But even they failed. God did not take that as an excuse to slight men and women or to become inaccessible to them. He was not hurt or wounded to the degree that He would shut man out entirely. Instead, His HEART made provision for a better and more sure way; and, in time, He gave us a better Priest, One who was perfect and Who would never fail.

For we do not have a high priest who is unable to sympathize with our weaknesses, but we have one who has been tempted in every way, just as we are—yet was without sin. Let us then approach the throne of grace with confidence, so that we may receive mercy and find grace to help us in our time of need.

Hebrews 4:15-16

We have nothing to fear. Jesus has faced all the disappointments of life and overcome them. He became acquainted with every heartache and every sorrow known to man. Yet He overcame them all. He faced all the temptations of life to which we are subjected by the Enemy, yet He remained true to His Father. What a wonderful and perfect Priest we have! We are overcomers through Him.

God's HEART is longsuffering.

The justice of God is based on the fact that everyone be given fair and undeniable treatment. His love demands it. He even listens to those who have arrayed themselves against Him.

Perhaps you have heard of instances where someone in anger has defied God and challenged Him — thinking in this way to prove His existence. They might shake their fists towards the sky, or utter profane words and railing accusations against the sovereignty of God. Personally, I have never seen God react in anger to this type of challenge. His HEART is bigger than that. He is not quick to judge. He doesn't jump at the chance to punish. He is *"patient," "longsuffering."*

> *The Lord is not slow in keeping his promise, as some understand slowness. He is patient with you, not wanting anyone to perish, but everyone to come to repentance.*
>
> 2 Peter 3:9

> *The Lord is not slack concerning his promise, as some men count slackness; but is longsuffering to us-ward, not willing that any should perish but that all should come to repentance.*
>
> 2 Peter 3:9 (KJV)

God's patience and longsuffering originate in His compassionate HEART. He finds more pleasure in showing mercy than in executing judgment. These thoughts can come only from a bountiful HEART with pure motives.

Another word the Bible uses to describe God's HEART is *"forbearance."*

God's HEART is full of forbearance.

The Greek word for forbearance is *anecho.* It means *forbear, put up with, a suspension of wrath.* (15) Although man may be sinful, and judgment may be due and inevitable, God has another concern. He does everything possible to delay, hold back, and even suspend wrath. His hope is that we will turn to Him in repentance and live.

> *Or do you show contempt for the riches of his kindness, tolerance and patience, not realizing that God's kindness leads you toward repentance?*
>
> Romans 2:4

> *And are justified freely by his grace through the redemption that came by Christ Jesus. God presented him as a sacrifice of atonement, through faith in his blood. He did this to demonstrate his justice, because in his forbearance he had left the sins committed beforehand unpunished.*
>
> Romans 3:24-25

Some people are convinced that fear is the greatest motivation of man for repentance and submission to the will of God. Those people don't know God very well. He would rather lead His people through grace, the unmerited favor of God. His great forbearance forbids that He deal with us according to our sins. He rather deals with us according to His HEART of compassion and His knowledge of what we can be, not what we are at the moment or what we have done in the past.

The concept of God's forbearance is not new. It is as old as the human race. When Adam, that first specimen of mankind, was disobedient to His Creator and, with his wife, succumbed to the lies of Satan and partook of the tree of the knowledge of good and evil, he immediately felt the weight of his sin and the sense of his fractured relationship with God. He hid himself.

God knew what Adam had done, yet He could not leave him there in hiding, without an attempt to heal the rift. He visited Adam's garden, as before.

But the Lord God called to the man, "Where are you?"
Genesis 3:9

This was not the voice of a demanding Sovereign, anxious to repay man for his wrong doing. This was the voice of a compassionate and forbearing HEART, always seeking a restoration of broken relationships. God cares about His wounded creation.

When Abraham interceded for the wicked cities of Sodom and Gomorrah, God listened.

"Lord, if I can find fifty righteous people in those cities, will you spare them?"

When God agreed, Abraham grew more bold.

"If I can find forty righteous people, will you spare them?"

"If I can find thirty righteous people, will you spare them?"

"If I can find twenty righteous people, will you spare them?"

When God agreed, Abraham made one last plea:

> *Then he said, "May the Lord not be angry, but let me speak just once more. What if only ten can be found there?"*
> *He answered, "For the sake of ten, I will not destroy it."*
>
> Genesis 18:32

We serve a wonderfully compassionate God. His love has no bounds. He never delights in judgment. He delights in mercy.

Jonah was angry when God didn't destroy Nineveh, as he had been sent to prophesy. But God was more concerned about a great city which had repented and turned to him than about the hurt pride of His prophet.

> *"But Nineveh has more than a hundred and twenty thousand people who cannot tell their right hand from their left, and many cattle as well. Should I not be concerned about that great city?"*
>
> Jonah 4:11

Those priests of Nehemiah's day speak to our generation, as well. As they were praying to God and confessing their sins and the sins of their people, God used them to speak words that every generation needs to hear.

> *For many years you were patient with them. By your Spirit you admonished them through your prophets. Yet they paid no attention, so you handed them over to the neighboring peoples.*
>
> Nehemiah 9:30

Judgment is God's last resort. His compassionate HEART demands that He make every possible effort to rescue man before it comes to that. Reluctantly, He permits judgment—when all else fails. What a compassionate and just God we serve!

His love for us requires that He enter into covenant with us, that He make a commitment, a promise to us.

In the traditional wedding ceremony, powerful words of commitment are used. Among them, none is more powerful than the phrase: *"so long as you both shall live."* This is the anticipated length of duration of a marriage agreement between two caring and loving hearts. At the moment those vows are taken, there is no doubt that the devotion necessary to fulfill the vow is present.

However, we all know what often happens. The old adage is still true: *"A wedding takes only about an hour, but a marriage takes a lifetime."* As time goes on, some unknowns creep into the marriage equation. The sailing becomes choppy, and the waters often become unnavigable. In these all-too-frequent cases, the marriage craft gets tossed about and occasionally becomes shipwrecked.

What has happened? The initial intent of the vowing parties was accurate and sincere. They fully intended for their love to last "as long as [*they*] both [*would*] live." It was not a foolish promise, but a noble one, worthy of keeping. Yet, in the end, the marriage failed.

These days some couples have opted to make prenuptial agreements, contracts, specifying what exactly will happen if the love both parties now feel diminishes or vanishes altogether and they decide to part ways.

The HEART of man is so changeable, so limited in its scope. Thank God that His HEART is not as ours. He is a God of total commitment for all time. His record is phenomenal. His promises are steadfast and sure. He has never broken a commitment and never will. His HEART never veers from its commitment.

His greatest promise to us is eternal life.

And this is what he promised us—even eternal life.
1 John 2:25

God has so much love for us that it will take all eternity for Him to display it fully. The little jump start we get here is just a beginning of His commitment to us, a commitment that will be just as real ten thousand years from now as it is today.

Those who know God, understand that His promises are unfailing because His compassionate HEART is unfailing and unchanging.

> *"Praise be to the Lord, who has given rest to his people Israel just as he promised. Not one word has failed of all the good promises he gave through his servant Moses."*
>
> 1 Kings 8:56

God's loving commitment to us is backed by divine authority and divine ability.

> *Being fully persuaded that God had power to do what he had promised.*
>
> Romans 4:21

Our loving and compassionate heavenly Father has a wonderful plan for each of us. He has destined us to "participate in the divine nature."

> *Through these he has given us his very great and precious promises, so that through them you may participate in the divine nature and escape the corruption in the world caused by evil desires.*
>
> 2 Peter 1:4

Despite our failures and weaknesses, He does not cast us aside, but prepares for us a glorious future. He has destined us to *"escape the corruption in the world caused by evil desires."*

He can make a perfect HEART because His HEART is perfect. Why not allow Him to give you a fresh jump start today.

Chapter 7

His Strong ARM

"Listen to me, my people;
hear me, my nation:
The law will go out from me;
my justice will become a light to the nations.
My righteousness draws near speedily,
my salvation is on the way,
and my ARM will bring justice to the nations.
The islands will look to me
and wait in hope for my ARM.
Lift up your eyes to the heavens,
look at the earth beneath;
the heavens will vanish like smoke,
the earth will wear out like a garment
and its inhabitants die like flies
But my salvation will last forever,
my righteousness will never fail.

"Hear me, you who know what is right,
you people who have my law in your hearts:

Do not fear the reproach of men
or be terrified by their insults.
For the moth will eat them up like a garment;
the worm will devour them like wool.
But my righteousness will last forever,
my salvation through all generations."

Awake, awake! Clothe yourself with strength, O ARM of the Lord;
awake, as in days gone by, as in generations of old.
Was it not you who cut Rahab to pieces,
who pierced that monster through?
Was it not you who dried up the sea,
the waters of the great deep,
who made a road in the depths of the sea
so that the redeemed might cross over?
The ransomed of the Lord will return.
They will enter Zion with singing;
everlasting joy will crown their heads.
Gladness and joy will overtake them,
and sorrow and sighing will flee away.

"I, even I, am he who comforts you.
Who are you that you fear mortal men,
the sons of men, who are but grass.

Isaiah 51:4-12

God's strong ARM is an instrument of His Divine provision and His Divine protection.

When we think of ARMS, the first thing that comes to mind is hugging. I am convinced that hugging is the most important duty of the arms. That's why I love that bumper sticker that says: *"Hugs, not Drugs!"* Unfortunately, when young people get seriously involved in drugs, it is often too late for hugs. But it doesn't hurt to try. We all need to be loved.

God has a lot of good hugs waiting for every eager believer. His hugs are comforting and restorative. Because His ARMS are so strong, being in His ARMS brings us an indescribable sense of security. Nothing could be more important.

Once, when I had been away for a time, I was enjoying some special hugs from my wife, when a tiny voice interrupted and said, "Mom, what are you doing hugging my friend Jim?" It was our five-year-old. She was impatiently awaiting her turn. I had become her "friend" because she had known my arms in times of hurt or sickness. But we didn't need special occasions to hug. We did it regularly to show our special affection for one another and to lend loving reassurance.

I believe that we are living in a time when the whole of creation will soon long to be in the ARMS of Almighty God. The world will soon cry out to be God's friend. And, as always, His loving ARMS will be outstretched in eager anticipation.

The ARM of the Lord is simple by definition. The Hebrew word is *zero'a* and means *the power, strength and help afforded by the Almighty.* The ARMS of the Lord not only are available for hugging. His ARMS draw us toward Him and offer His strength, His power, and His help.

His strong ARM has been demonstrated on behalf of His people down through the centuries.

It was God's mighty ARM which brought Israel out of Egypt.

> *Has any god ever tried to take for himself one nation out of another nation, by testings, by miraculous signs and wonders, by war, by a mighty hand and an outstretched ARM, or by great and awesome deeds, like all the things the Lord your God did for you in Egypt before your very eyes?*
>
> Deuteronomy 4:34

> *Remember that you were slaves in Egypt and that the Lord your God brought you out of there with a mighty hand and an outstretched ARM. Therefore the Lord your God has commanded you to observe the Sabbath day.*
>
> Deuteronomy 5:15

You saw with your own eyes the great trials, the miraculous signs and wonders, the mighty hand and outstretched ARM, with which the Lord your God brought you out. The Lord your God will do the same to all the peoples you now fear.

Deuteronomy 7:19

Looking back at Moses' day, we might say, "That was very nice." But the important thing is to know that the strong ARM of our God has not changed. If He could deliver Moses and all Israel from the Pharaoh and from Egypt, He can deliver us from whatever we face in the closing years of the twentieth century. When we pray, we must catch a vision of His mighty ARM, ready to deliver us. What confidence this knowledge inspires!

We all agree that we are living in a very difficult time. In a world of so much disagreement, there is agreement on that one thing:

> The Theologian says we are racing towards Armageddon.
> The Scientist says we are racing towards Armageddon.
> The Politician says we are racing towards Armageddon.
> The Pacifist says we are racing towards Armageddon.
> The Revolutionist says we are racing towards Armageddon.
> The Environmentalist says that we are racing towards Armageddon.
> The Military Strategist says that we are racing towards Armageddon.

Everyone seems to agree on the problem, but no one seems to have a solution. With all the "experts" available to us, the solution seems more distant than ever. We can agree that:

A new scientific discovery would cause man to marvel, but it wouldn't solve his problems.

A new political party would probably enlist many of man's energies but would not provide him with the satisfaction for which he is longing.

A new peaceful coalition among the peoples of the world would excite many but would do little to settle the unrest in the masses.

A new revolution would certainly change things drastically but not more than any other revolt of the past.

A new environment would be nice for a while, but man would quickly find ways to pollute it.

A new military regime would abolish the old order but would not necessarily establish a new one.

A new religion won't resolve our problems either.

Long ago God declared that He would prevail by His mighty ARM and that those who trusted His ARM would also prevail. The same might which was demonstrated in Egypt will be demonstrated by the ARM of the Lord in these last days.

Isaiah knew the importance of the ARM of the Lord. He used this expression twelve times in his writings. His prayer reflects his insight into the power of God's ARM.

O Lord, be gracious unto us; we have waited for thee: be thou their ARM every morning, our salvation also in the time of trouble.

Isaiah 33:2 (KJV)

Isaiah further declared:

See, the Sovereign Lord comes with power,
and his ARM rules for him.
See, his reward is with him,
and his recompense accompanies him.
He tends his flock like a shepherd:
He gathers the lambs in his arms
and carries them close to his heart;
he gently leads those that have young.

Isaiah 40:10-11

Several times I have seen the "World Wrist Wrestling Tournaments" on television. They are amazing.

Two men come to center stage of a specially designed platform. Their muscles bulge beneath their shirts. Considerable time is spent jockeying for position. Each finger and thumb must be in perfect position. When this posturing is completed, an awesome display of human strength begins. Eventually, when one of the men is able to bend the other's ARM backward to a "pin" position, he is declared the winner.

Life is a lot like that tournament. All the forces of evil spend their considerable energies trying to get man "pinned." Each of us has experienced some defeats, some disappointments, some distractions of purpose and even some disgrace. Like those ARM wrestlers, we have longed for some steroid that will make us stronger, something that will give us bulk and mass, and allow us to come out the winner—for once.

I have good news for you. God sees all our struggles and is extending His mighty ARM to rescue us from those forces that seek to destroy us. He wants to become our coach and strategist. We must be willing to take His advice and work toward His goals. That is why He said through Isaiah:

> *"Listen to me, my people; hear me, my nation: The law will go out from me."*
>
> Isaiah 51:4

Our own efforts have proven meaningless. Why not give God a chance? Why not listen to what He has to say? Why not trust His strength. If He has never failed, why should we expect Him to fail now?

Aren't you tired of being overpowered by the enemy? Aren't you tired of stumbling through life as a failure? God wants to change all that. He wants to manifest His strength in your behalf. He wants to make you a winner. Listen to Him. Accept His "law."

How wonderful it is to have a coach who has never lost a battle! He loves us and has our best interests at heart. He knows what He is doing. Give Him a chance with your life. Hear Him.

The strength of His ARM is established, therefore the future is determined. Be sure you are on the right team.

The world doesn't have the answers we need. When will the church stop looking to the world for answers? When a child needs comforting, it never rushes to the arms of a stranger. What does a stranger know? Run to Father's arms.

In those "World Wrist Wrestling Tournaments" before each individual contest begins, the ARM wrestlers do everything they can to do a "psyche job" on their opponents, to intimidate them. They muster up ferocious looks on their faces and stare defiantly into their opponents eyes. It seems to work.

God knows how to intimidate the enemy too. He does it another way. He tells us to look up, to see the glories of His heavens, to see the glories of His creation on the earth, to see the work of His hands and to know that He can destroy it all in a moment.

Lift up your eyes to the heavens, look at the earth beneath; the heavens will vanish like smoke, the earth will wear out like a garment and its inhabitants die like flies. But my salvation will last forever, my righteousness will never fail.

Isaiah 51:6

Understanding the strength of God's ARM inspires confidence in calling out to Him for help in time of need.

Awake, awake! Clothe yourself with strength, O ARM of the Lord; awake, as in days gone by, as in generations of old.

Isaiah 51:8-9

God knows when the battle is heating up. He knows when the signal is about to be given. He knows the moment in which you will need optimum strength. And He is standing by, ready to hear your cry.

Why do we always try to settle everything ourselves? It never works. Why do we lean on our own understand and trust in our own wisdom? We always fail. Give God a chance to make something of your life. He has destined you to be champions.

The ARM of the Lord is fully manifested in the Person and works of Jesus. When we trust Him completely, the Lord does awake, *"as in the former days."*

We all relish the thought of having the experiences of the "old time religion." And we can. The secret of experiencing the "old time religion" is to return to the old time trust in God, the author of those experiences. He hasn't changed at all. He is still the same, as the Scriptures declare.

> *Jesus Christ is the same yesterday and today and forever.*
>
> Hebrews 13:8

In order to work for us, God must be Lord of our lives. We must make Him Lord. He will not take that position by force. The choice is ours. Let Him take charge. Trust His competence.

The full authority of the God-head is vested in the Person of Jesus. In Him, the ARM of the Lord, (His strength, power and help) is readily available to us, just as it was in Moses' day.

The writer of the Book of Hebrews put it this way:

But we see Jesus, who was made a little lower than the angels for the suffering of death, crowned with glory and honour; that he by the grace of God should taste death for every man. For it became him, for whom are all things, and by whom are all things, in bringing many sons unto glory, to make THE CAPTAIN OF THEIR SALVATION perfect through sufferings.

Hebrews 2:9-10 (KJV)

The Psalmist didn't have the privilege of living in New Testament times. He could not experience a Risen Savior by his side. Yet, he still recognized the strength in the ARM of The Lord.

Arise, O Lord, in your anger;
rise up against the rage of my enemies.
Awake, my God; decree justice.
Let the assembled peoples gather around you.
Rule over them from on high;
let the Lord judge the peoples.
Judge me, O Lord, according to my righteousness,
according to my integrity, O Most High.

Psalms 7:6-8

God's ARM is our sufficiency.

Not that we are sufficient of ourselves to think any thing as of ourselves; but our sufficiency is of God;

2 Corinthians 3:5 (KJV)

Because He is our sufficiency, we must never be detached from the vine, lest we become useless.

> *"I am the vine; you are the branches. If a man remains in me and I in him, he will bear much fruit; apart from me you can do nothing."*
>
> John 15:5

Because He is our sufficiency, we have no confidence in ourselves. The self confidence which the world is proclaiming as the resolution of every problem is our worst enemy.

> *For it is we who are the circumcision, we who worship by the Spirit of God, who glory in Christ Jesus, and who put no confidence in the flesh.*
>
> Philippians 3:3

We must learn to lean on the ARM of the LORD. Jesus is our example.

> *Jesus gave them this answer: "I tell you the truth, the Son can do nothing by himself; he can do only what he sees his Father doing, because whatever the Father does the Son also does."*
>
> John 5:19

> *By myself I can do nothing; I judge only as I hear, and my judgment is just, for I seek not to please myself but him who sent me.*
>
> John 5:30

> *So Jesus said, "When you have lifted up the Son of Man, then you will know that I am the one I claim to*

be and that I do nothing on my own but speak just what the Father has taught me."

John 8:28

If Jesus could do nothing on His own, how much more we should recognize our total dependence on the Father. We can become *"more than conquerors"*—if and when we learn to lean heavily upon God's strong ARM. As the ARM of the Lord never failed in the past, so His ARM will not fail us in these last days. Let Him be Lord of your life. It is worthwhile to surrender yourself fully to God's will and way.

Chapter 8

His Protective HAND

The Jews gathered around him, saying, "How long will you keep us in suspense? If you are the Christ, tell us plainly."
Jesus answered, "I did tell you, but you do not believe. The miracles I do in my Father's name speak for me, but you do not believe because you are not my sheep. My sheep listen to my voice; I know them, and they follow me. I give them eternal life, and they shall never perish; no one can snatch them out of my HAND. My Father, who has given them to me, is greater than all; no one can snatch them out of my Father's HAND. I and the Father are one."

John 10:24-30

Mary Magdalene went to the disciples with the news: "I have seen the Lord!" And she told them that he had said these things to her.
On the evening of that first day of the week, when the disciples were together, with the doors locked for fear

of the Jews, Jesus came and stood among them and said, "Peace be with you!" After he said this, he showed them his hands and side. The disciples were overjoyed when they saw the Lord.
Again Jesus said, "Peace be with you! As the Father has sent me, I am sending you." And with that he breathed on them and said, "Receive the Holy Spirit. If you forgive anyone his sins, they are forgiven; if you do not forgive them, they are not forgiven."
Now Thomas (called Didymus), one of the Twelve, was not with the disciples when Jesus came. So the other disciples told him, "We have seen the Lord!"
But he said to them, "Unless I see the nail marks in his hands and put my finger where the nails were, and put my HAND into his side, I will not believe it."
A week later his disciples were in the house again, and Thomas was with them. Though the doors were locked, Jesus came and stood among them and said, "Peace be with you!" Then he said to Thomas, "Put your finger here; see my hands. Reach out your HAND and put it into my side. Stop doubting and believe."
Thomas said to him, "My Lord and my God!"
John 20:18-28

How interesting! The proof which the disciples would accept of the fact that Christ had risen was to see His HANDS. Zechariah had prophesied of this:

And one shall say unto him, What are these wounds in thine hands? Then he shall answer, Those with which I was wounded in the house of my friends.
Zechariah 13:6 (KJV)

The word *HAND* appears nearly one thousand times in the Bible, with a variety of applications and illustrations. Because of that, there are many definitions of the word. The definition that concerns us here in John 10:28-29 is: "The hand of the Lord means the embodiment of divine power. God's hand indicates His wonderworking power in which He grants security and protection to all those who trust Him." (16)

Our own HANDS can be used in very different ways. Usually, when the palms of our HANDS are up and visible, we are using our hands for something tender and constructive: beckoning, supporting, or embracing, for example. When our palms are down or clenched, they are in an authoritative position for twisting, suppressing or even punching.

The depiction of God's HANDS in Scripture teach us much about His character.

His HANDS are caring and supportive.

"From Childhood, Albrecht Durer wanted to paint. Finally, he left home to study with a great artist. He met a friend who also had this same desire and the two became roommates. Both being poor, they found it difficult to make a living and study at the same time. Albrecht's friend offered to work while Albrecht studied. Then when the paintings began to sell, he would have his chance. After much persuasion, Albrecht agreed and worked faithfully while his friend toiled long hours to make a living.

"The day came when Albrecht sold a wood-carving and his friend went back to his paints, only to find that the hard work had stiffened and twisted his fingers and he could no longer paint with skill. When Albrecht learned what had happened to his friend, he was filled with great sorrow. One day returning home unexpectedly, he heard the voice of his friend and saw the gnarled, toilworn hands folded in prayer before him.

"'I can show the world my appreciation by painting his hands as I see them now, folded in prayer." It was this thought that inspired Albrecht Durer when he realized that he could never give back to his friend the skill which had left his hands.

"Durer's gratitude was captured in his inspired painting that has become world famous. And, we are blessed by both the beauty of the painting and the beautiful story of gratitude and brotherhood." (17)

Praying Hands is one of the best loved paintings ever done. It tells us a lot about God's love for a dying world. As Albrecht's friend sacrificed himself so that the painter could have success, Jesus gave His life on the cross so that we could have abundant and everlasting life. What greater expression of care and support for humanity could be possible?

His HANDS are sacrificial.

"During the Crusades, a knight was taken captive by the Moslem Saladin. The Knight begged for his life, claiming that he had a wife in England who loved him dearly. Saladin commented that she would soon forget him and marry another. On second thought, the cruel chieftain offered to set the man free if the lady in question would send her right HAND as a token of her love for this captive.

"When word was sent to this wife in England, she immediately cut off her right HAND and sent it to Saladin. The man was forthwith returned to England.

"There is a statue of this faithful woman in one of the old cathedrals of England. She is attractive, but the statue shows her without the right HAND." (18)

What a powerful testimony of the depth of her sacrificing spirit!

When God sent the world His Only Begotten Son, He placed Him in Mary's womb with sacrificial HANDS—and all for our benefit.

His HANDS are all-encompassing and engulfing.

"A gentleman once visited a great jewelry store, owned by a friend. His friend showed him magnificent diamonds, and other splendid stones. Amongst these stones his eye lighted on one that seemed quite lusterless, and, pointing to it, he said: 'That has no beauty at all."

"But his friend put it in the hollow of his hand, and shut his hand, and then in a few moments opened it again.

"What a surprise! The entire stone gleamed with all the splendours of the rainbow.

"What have you done to it?" asked the astonished gazer.

"His friend answered: 'This is an opal. It is what we call the sympathetic Jewel. It only needs to be gripped with the human HAND to bring out its wonderful beauty.' " (19)

In retrospect, life is like the opal. It is lusterless and absent of real beauty until it is shut up within the HAND of God. After God's HANDS have embraced it and transferred to it the warmth and joy of His love, only then it begins to transmit a radiant beauty that astonishes the beholder.

The HAND has been called "the executive officer of the brain." No other organ has such a variety of functions:

"To lend a HAND"	is an expression of service.
"To be a poor HAND"	is a definite condemnation.
"To be an old HAND"	is a mark of ripe experience.
"To come with empty HAND"	is an expression of poverty or leanness.
"To rule with a heavy HAND"	indicates an oppressor.

"To be a right HAND man"	is to be an able assistant, valued and capable.
"To get one's HAND in"	is to become familiar with the work.
"To take a thing in HAND"	is to make a serious undertaking.
"To act with a high HAND"	is an indication of arrogance.
"To have clean hands"	is to be incorruptible.
"To have your hands full"	is to be completely occupied.
"To be a handful"	is to be a nuisance.
"To wash one's hands"	is to abandon completely.
"All hands on deck"	is the cry in an hour of danger.
"Hands off"	is a serious warning not to be ignored.
"Hands up"	is an indication of surrender.
"A HAND out"	is request for something to be given freely.

I read of a man in England who was classified as a professional beggar. He could elaborate the most believable lies as he worked the streets of his city, panhandling. The thing that irritated the people who were taken in by his lies was that when his subjects would respond to his pleas, he would reach for their money with a HAND that had tattooed in the palm *"Thank you."*

God's HANDS represent His ultimate capability. They are different in both scope and design from the human HAND.

His HANDS are mighty.

As a young lad, I can very vividly remember climbing onto a building that I had been repeatedly warned to avoid. I had no problem getting up. But, when it came time to descend, I looked down toward the ground and panicked. I was so terrified that, after weighing all the consequences, I called for my father to come and help me. I knew I would get a spanking for disobeying him. But I was afraid not to call him.

He came. Climbing as high as he could, he reached out his HANDS to me. And when I saw his HANDS, I lost all fear and was able to move again, into the safety of his embrace. Interestingly enough, the same HANDS which rescued me from that building were soon used to spank me.

God's children were in Egypt's bondage because of disobedience. He delivered them and gave them a new law by which to live. Later, He reminded them:

Remember that you were slaves in Egypt and that the Lord your God brought you out of there with a mighty HAND and an outstretched arm. Therefore the Lord your God has commanded you to observe the Sabbath day.

Deuteronomy 5:15

After they had crossed over the Jordan River and were about to face Jericho and the giants of the promised land, He again reminded them:

"He did this so that all the peoples of the earth might know that the HAND of the Lord is powerful and so that you might always fear the Lord your God."

Joshua 4:24

The Psalmist praised God for the providence and care that He took over His people. He showed us that we need never despair in the midst of life's circumstances.

Your arm is endued with power; your HAND is strong, your right HAND exalted.

Psalms 89:13

Sing to the Lord a new song, for he has done marvelous things; his right HAND and his holy arm have worked salvation for him.

Psalms 98:1

The early apostles understood the power of God's HAND.

Humble yourselves, therefore, under God's mighty HAND, that he may lift you up in due time.

1 Peter 5:6

His are HANDS of chastening.

God is a merciful God. Yet He is a just God. The one truth cannot cancel the other. Mercy and justice go together. When God sees something that is impeding the spiritual progress of His people, it displeases Him and causes Him to react. Love demands it.

Ashdod was one of five principle cities of the Philistines. It was also the seat of worship of their ancient fish god, Dagon. When the Philistines defeated Israel at Ebenezer and captured the Ark of the Covenant (Israel's most holy shrine because God's presence dwelt there), the pagans took the Ark into Dagon's Temple. In this way, they hoped to profane the Ark and demoralize the people of Israel. The plan backfired.

The Lord's HAND was heavy upon the people of Ashdod and its vicinity; he brought devastation upon them and afflicted them with tumors.

1 Samuel 5:6

The same tender, outstretched and loving HAND of God is capable of punishing that which tries to interfere with His people coming closer to Him.

In Paul's time, a deputy governor, Sergius Paulus, had a desire to hear the truth of the Gospel which he and Barnabas were preaching and teaching. Elymus the sorcerer wanted to prevent that eventuality and keep the man in darkness. His plan backfired, as well.

Then Saul, who was also called Paul, filled with the Holy Spirit, looked straight at Elymas and said, "You are a child of the devil and an enemy of everything that is right! You are full of all kinds of deceit and trickery. Will you never stop perverting the right ways of the Lord? Now the HAND of the Lord is against you. You are going to be blind, and for a time you will be unable to see the light of the sun." Immediately mist and darkness came over him, and he groped about, seeking someone to lead him by the HAND.

Acts 13:9-11

His are HANDS of blessing.

God not only gets us out of trouble; He keeps us from getting into so much trouble. When we look back and see the things that could have happened to us, it is a wonder that any of us made it this far. Thank God that He has been so good to us.

Even when we did slip and fall, and when total tragedy seemed imminent, God's HAND was there and intervened on our behalf. God's HAND is a HAND of blessing.

The steps of a good man are ordered by the Lord: and he delighteth in his way. Though he fall, he shall not be utterly cast down: for the Lord upholdeth him with his HAND.

Psalms 37:23-24 (KJV)

We are safe in the HANDS of God. He said, *"no one can snatch them out of my HAND"* (John 10:28). Then He confirmed this truth by repeating, *"...no one can snatch them out of my Father's HAND"* (Verse 29).

His hands are outstretched to you today. Why not put your HAND into His?

Chapter 9

His Precise FINGER

O Lord, our Lord,
how majestic is your name in all the earth!
You have set your glory above the heavens.
From the lips of children and infants
you have ordained praise
because of your enemies,
to silence the foe and the avenger.

When I consider your heavens,
the work of your FINGERS,
the moon and the stars,
which you have set in place,
what is man that you are mindful of him,
the son of man that you care for him?
You made him a little lower than the heavenly beings
and crowned him with glory and honor.

You made him ruler over the works of your hands;
you put everything under his feet:

all flocks and herds,
and the beasts of the field,
the birds of the air,
and the fish of the sea,
all that swim the paths of the seas.
O Lord, our Lord,
how majestic is your name in all the earth!

Psalms 8:1-9

The *FINGER is the instrument of precision, the segment of the hand that is designed for deliberate* and *thorough action.* Many English phrases use the word.

1. To burn one's FINGER is to cause oneself trouble by being too inquisitive or meddlesome.
2. To have a FINGER in the pie is to help do something or to participate.
3. To have one's FINGERS crossed is to hope for or against something.
4. To lift a FINGER is to make the slightest effort.
5. To put one's FINGER on is to indicate or ascertain exactly.
6. To put the FINGER on is to identify or to inform.
7. A FINGER board is the neck of a violin or other stringed instrument.
8. A FINGER bowl is a small bowl for rinsing FINGERS at the table after a meal.

9. A FINGER breadth is a measurement of about ¾ to one inch.

There is also a *FINGER* mark, *FINGER* print, *FINGER* nail, *FINGER* paint, a *FINGER tip, a FINGER* wave, etc.

The FINGER is a very identifiable organ. The F.B.I have records of over 60 Million FINGERprints which take up 160 million files. They receive an average of 24,000 additional FINGERprints every day.

We know how important our FINGERS are to us. We use them for almost everything. God's FINGER also has many uses. It is used for surgery, for separating, for hand-crafting and for deliverance. The use of His FINGER reveals the wonderful thought process behind His every action.

> *In the beginning was the Word, and the Word was with God, and the Word was God.*
>
> John 1:1

Word in the Greek is *logos*. It means *the complete realm of thought*. Everything that God's FINGERS performed in creation was the result of His marvelous thought processes. His thoughts control the preciseness of His FINGERS.

It is amazing to watch ladies who knit. Their FINGERS fly. And those FINGERS cannot just move any way they like; they must move in precise patterns. In her mind that lady has a picture of a garment. She knows how it will look: the color, the size, the pattern. It is so real to her that she is even anticipating the joy it will bring to the person who will receive it. Those thoughts make the FINGERS fly, and what those FINGERS do becomes the "bottom line" of her activity.

In a sense, the FINGER of God is the bottom line of God's dealings with man—for good or evil. Like the hand, the FINGER can bless or it can chasten. No one likes to have a FINGER pointed at them in judgment. They would prefer to have it work to their advantage.

Charlemagne, the emperor of the Holy Roman Empire from 800 A.D. until 814 A.D., gave specific instructions on how he should be buried when his time came. He wanted to be buried seated in the royal posture of a monarch on his throne. Also he directed that a copy of the Gospels be placed upon his knees, his sword beside him, the imperial crown on his head, and the royal mantle of empire on his shoulders.

Charlemagne died and was buried in accordance with his wishes. For 180 years he remained untouched. About 1000 A.D., his tomb was opened by the Emperor Otho. He found the skeleton of Charlemagne, "dissolved and dismembered into various hideous postures." The skull was still wearing the crown. The robe and mantle had virtually deteriorated, the sword had rusted, and one of Charlemagne's decayed FINGERS had fallen across the Scriptures and was pointing to this verse:

> *What good will it be for a man if he gains the whole world, yet forfeits his soul? Or what can a man give in exchange for his soul?*
>
> Matthew 16:26

"The various relics were collected and used in the coronation of the emperors of Germany to signify their greatness and succession from Charlemagne." (20)

The term the FINGER of God was first used by the magicians of Pharaoh's court. When God began to deal with Pharaoh about letting His people go, Pharaoh hardened his heart and refused. One by one Egypt experienced a series of plagues.

> *Then the Lord said to Moses, "Tell Aaron, 'Stretch out your staff and strike the dust of the ground,' and throughout the land of Egypt the dust will become gnats."*
>
> *They did this, and when Aaron stretched out his hand with the staff and struck the dust of the ground, gnats came upon men and animals. All the dust throughout the land of Egypt became gnats. But when the magicians tried to produce gnats by their secret arts, they could not. And the gnats were on men and animals.*
>
> *The magicians said to Pharaoh, "This is the FINGER of God." But Pharaoh's heart was hard and he would not listen, just as the Lord had said.*
>
> Exodus 8:16-19

Although the magicians seem to have initiated the expression, it was one which the people of God came to love and respect through the years. The FINGER of God meant disaster to His foes but, to His children, it was a reflection of His genuine concern for their welfare.

The FINGER of God commands and guides.

After the Lord delivered His people from Egypt and set them on their journey toward the promised land, He took Moses aside one day on a mountain to commune with him. While Moses was there on the mountain, God gave him the law, written on tablets of stone with His own FINGER.

> *When the Lord finished speaking to Moses on Mount Sinai, he gave him the two tablets of the Testimony, the tablets of stone inscribed by the FINGER of God.*
>
> Exodus 31:18

Chapter 32, gives us more detail:

> *Moses turned and went down the mountain with the two tablets of the Testimony in his hands. They were inscribed on both sides, front and back. The tablets were the work of God; the writing was the writing of God, engraved on the tablets.*
>
> Exodus 32:15-16

Because of the lightning on the mountain and the quaking, some supposed that God wrote on the tables of stone with lightning.

Mount Sinai was covered with smoke, because the Lord descended on it in fire. The smoke billowed up from it like smoke from a furnace, the whole mountain trembled violently,

Exodus 19:18

Moses, who was the only person actually present on the mountain at the time, said that God did it with His FINGER. The holy thoughts of God and His desires for the future well-being of His people caused His FINGERS to fly. With them He set a standard of conduct that would be a focal point of law for those who loved Him in the future. It was never to be forgotten, even in times of prosperity.

When the Lord your God brings you into the land he swore to your fathers, to Abraham, Isaac and Jacob, to give you—a land with large, flourishing cities you did not build, houses filled with all kinds of good things you did not provide, wells you did not dig, and vineyards and olive groves you did not plant—then when you eat and are satisfied, be careful that you do not forget the Lord, who brought you out of Egypt, out of the land of slavery.
Fear the Lord your God, serve him only and take your oaths in his name.

Deuteronomy 6:10-13

What God wrote with His FINGER would guide His people into the promised land, literally and spiritually. His FINGER still points the way.

The FINGER of God delivers.

When the Pharisees began to tempt Jesus, He used the term *the FINGER* of God against them. He had just finished teaching His disciples the three-fold principle of prayer.

> ASK: *"Ask and it will be given to you."*
> SEEK: *"Seek and you will find."*
> KNOCK: *"Knock and the door will be opened to you."* Luke 11:9

He had cast out a demon (Verse 14); and because of that not everyone was happy with Him.

> *But some of them said, "By Beelzebub, the prince of demons, he is driving out demons."*
>
> Luke 11:15

Taking authority over demons has always been controversial. It was then that the people began to find ways to tempt (test) Him. Finally, He silenced their arguments.

> *Jesus knew their thoughts and said to them: "Any kingdom divided against itself will be ruined, and a house divided against itself will fall. If Satan is divided against himself, how can his kingdom stand? I say this because you claim that I drive out demons by Beelzebub. Now if I drive out demons by Beelzebub, by whom do your followers drive them out? So then, they will be your judges. But if I drive out demons by the FINGER of God, then the kingdom of God has come to you.*
>
> Luke 11:17-20

Jesus drove out demons "by the FINGER of God." Matthew relates the same occurrence in this way:

But if I drive out demons by the Spirit of God, then the kingdom of God has come upon you.

Matthew 12:28

It wasn't a physical FINGER. It was a spiritual metaphor. The FINGER of God is the unseen yet visibly witnessed moving of the Spirit of God which brings about our deliverance from harmful and threatening things in our lives. It is the precise movement of God in a situation in which God steps in to act on our behalf, demonstrating in the process His miraculous power and ability.

During the time of Daniel there was another account of the miraculous use of God's FINGERS. One night in Belshazzar's banquet hall, while the king and all his princes were drinking their wine and praising their gods, the Scriptures say:

As they drank the wine, they praised the gods of gold and silver, of bronze, iron, wood and stone.
Suddenly the FINGERS of a human hand appeared and wrote on the plaster of the wall, near the lampstand in the royal palace. The king watched the hand as it wrote. His face turned pale and he was so frightened that his knees knocked together and his legs gave way.
The king called out for the enchanters, astrologers and diviners to be brought and said to these wise men of

Babylon, "Whoever reads this writing and tells me what it means will be clothed in purple and have a gold chain placed around his neck, and he will be made the third highest ruler in the kingdom."

Daniel 5:4-7

In the face of man's rebelliousness against God and his pursuit of his own selfish ways, God writes on the wall a message of conviction. He is faithful to remind man of his sinful ways and of their damning consequence. It often has no impact whatsoever, but God is faithful to warn us nevertheless.

During His earthly ministry, Jesus used the FINGER of God to bring thousands of men and women relief from their torments and to set them free from their physical maladies. Some of those thousands were impacted spiritually. Many were not. He was crucified by His detractors.

God was obviously disappointed with the lack of response on the part of those who heard the teachings of Jesus and witnessed His miracles. He did not give up, however, on the human race. He made an even greater covenant with us.

Because by one sacrifice he has made perfect forever those who are being made holy.
The Holy Spirit also testifies to us about this. First he says:
"This is the covenant I will make with them
after that time, says the Lord.

I will put my laws in their hearts,
and I will write them on their minds."

Then he adds:

"Their sins and lawless acts
I will remember no more."

Hebrews 10:14-17

God's greatest desire is to write His laws, by the invisible, spiritual FINGER of God, upon the hearts and minds of men and women, to indelibly etch them into our memories. This will give us the strength and confidence to live a life that is victorious over sin.

Then we will be able to say, like David of old:

O Lord, our Lord,
how majestic is your name in all the earth!
You have set your glory above the heavens.
From the lips of children and infants
you have ordained praise
because of your enemies,
to silence the foe and the avenger.

When I consider your heavens,
the work of your FINGERS,
the moon and the stars,
which you have set in place,
what is man that you are mindful of him,
the son of man that you care for him?

Psalms 8:1-4

Chapter 10

His Glorious FEET

"The glory of Lebanon will come to you, the pine, the fir and the cypress together, to adorn the place of my sanctuary; and I will glorify the place of my FEET."

Isaiah 60:13

This is what the Lord says: "Heaven is my throne, and the earth is my footstool. Where is the house you will build for me? Where will my resting place be?"

Isaiah 66:1

The concept of the FEET of God has its roots in the earliest beginnings of man's exposure to His Creator.

When God created man and placed him in the garden, He gave him a few simple instructions and then left him on his own. Adam soon proved that he was a self-willed creature. He had to have his own way. He chose to violate the simple principles that God had laid down and to give himself to the subversive spirit of the devil. Even then, God was not as angry with

Adam and Eve as He was with the serpent who beguiled them. He pronounced terrible judgment on the beast.

> *And I will put enmity between you and the woman, and between your offspring and hers; he will crush your head, and you will strike his heel."*
>
> Genesis 3:15

No sooner was the damage done than the remedy was revealed. God was not defeated. He cannot be defeated. And He does not forget those who try to defeat Him. He also does not take the defeat of His people lightly. Like any other parent, when something adverse happens to His children, He methodically goes to work, making the enemy pay for the damage done. The prophet Nahum expressed it well.

> *The Lord is slow to anger and great in power; the Lord will not leave the guilty unpunished. His way is in the whirlwind and the storm, and clouds are the dust of his FEET.*
>
> Nahum 1:3

In his attack upon Adam and Eve in the garden, Satan not only corrupted mankind, but he also corrupted the earth in which man was to dwell. This also displeased God. That day He declared war on all ungodliness and on all satanic influences and declared that He would one day bring this rebellious and sinful world into subjection. Our triumphant God will ultimately trample all of Satan's endeavors under his FEET.

> *For he must reign until he has put all his enemies UNDER HIS FEET.*
>
> 1 Corinthians 15:25

As with everything else in our God, this is so sure to happen that it is already counted as an accomplished fact.

> *And God placed all things UNDER HIS FEET and appointed him to be head over everything for the church.*
>
> Ephesians 1:22

As children of God, everything will one day also be put under our feet.

> *The God of peace will soon crush Satan UNDER YOUR FEET. The grace of our Lord Jesus be with you.*
>
> Romans 16:20

In the same way as Jesus' reign over everyone and everything is counted as an accomplished fact, our own future is so secure that God speaks of our ultimate reign as an accomplished fact—although it will become a physical reality sometime in the near future.

> *"What is man that you are mindful of him, the son of man that you care for him? You made him a little lower than the angels; you crowned him with glory and honor and put everything UNDER HIS*

FEET." In putting everything under him, God left nothing that is not subject to him. Yet at present we do not see everything subject to him.

Hebrews 2:6-8

God's will ultimately prevails. We are on the winning side.

When the disciples asked Jesus to teach them to pray, He answered:

"This, then, is how you should pray:

" 'Our Father in heaven,
hallowed be your name,
your kingdom come,
your will be done
on earth as it is in heaven.'"

Matthew 6:9-10

The highest will of the heavenly Father is that He reign here on the earth in the same way that He reigns in Heaven, that His power and holiness influence and control everything and everyone. And it will happen. Our God will reign. All things will be put UNDER HIS FEET.

The humiliation of Jesus during His time on the earth included His FEET.

Dogs have surrounded me; a band of evil men has encircled me, they have pierced my hands and my FEET.

Psalms 22:16

As Jesus hung on the cross, His FEET were just above eye level and were the part of Him most visible to those who witnessed the events of that fateful day.

When wicked men crucified Him, they were attempting to put an end to His power and authority. Little could they know that those humiliated FEET would one day rule all things. Exiled on the isle of Patmos, John saw a vision of the humiliated Christ. But he did not see Him in defeat. He saw Him coming in glory and power, to the dismay of His enemies.

> *Look, he is coming with the clouds, and every eye will see him, even those who pierced him; and all the peoples of the earth will mourn because of him. So shall it be! Amen.*
>
> Revelation 1:7

Death could not keep Him. The grave could not hold Him. Jesus is Lord over all and will reign—whatever men or devils might do.

Judas lifted his FOOT against His Master. Jesus predicted that it would happen.

> *"I am not referring to all of you; I know those I have chosen. But this is to fulfill the scripture: 'He who shares my bread has lifted up his heel against me.' "*
>
> John 13:18

Judas became an instrument of Satan's disloyalty to God, which started in heaven. Because of his disloyalty Satan had to be expelled. He did not, however, cease his hostilities. As soon as God had created man and placed him in the splendor of Eden, Satan felt like he had to intrude on that idyllic scene and sow seeds of disloyalty in man. From that moment he has not ceased, through every dispensation and every generation, to flaunt his rebellious nature and to work to build his army of malcontents. But, just as he cast Satan out of heaven, God cannot permit Him to run rampant on the earth forever. This will soon end.

Heaven belongs to God, and Satan cannot dwell there. But the earth also belongs to Him. As heaven is His throne, earth is His footstool. And He will reign here, as well.

As He set out to reign from the beginning, He will reign, and those who have elected to be His enemies will meet His wrath. His FOOT will tread on all disobedience and upon everything that Satan has disrupted and polluted. He will place everything once again under His FEET and establish the righteousness He ordained from the beginning.

Zechariah foresaw that day:

A day of the Lord is coming when your plunder will be divided among you.
Then the Lord will go out and fight against those nations, as he fights in the day of battle.

Zechariah 14:1 & 3

The total fulfillment of the prophecy of God's seed bruising the serpent's head will happen at this time and in this place—Jerusalem, the spot where Christ prayed and surrendered to the will of the Father for the test of mankind. Now Our Mighty Creator and Lord of Hosts will come back to strike a final blow to disloyalty and rebelliousness. All enemies will be put UNDER HIS FEET; and He will reign forever and ever.

In this knowledge, you and I can find great consolation. We can know without a doubt that:

When iniquity abounds and the love of many waxes cold, God is still in control.

When nation rises against nation and we hear of wars and rumors of wars, God will still be in control.

When famines and earthquakes and pestilences seem out of control, our God will still have the whole world in His hands.

When perilous times come and men become lovers of themselves—covetous, boastful, proud, arrogant, blasphemers, disobedient to parents, unthankful, unholy, without natural affection, false accusers, discontent, and despisers of those who are good—we need not be troubled. God hasn't changed His plan. He is still in control, and He will reign forever.

When there seem to be more sick days than well days, that doesn't change God. He is still reigning.

When this world demonstrates its arrogance against the Almighty, that doesn't change a thing. He still reigns.

When there seems to be more confusion than confidence, we will be at peace, knowing that He is still in charge.

When there seems to be more darkness than light, we will not be troubled. He still reigns.

When there seems to be more to pray about than to praise about, that doesn't change Him. He will make the place of His FEET glorious. Everything that opposes the perfect will of God will ultimately be subdued. In that day, those who have loved and served Him will humbly bow at His FEET and worship Him Who has always been Lord of Lord and King of Kings, Creator of the Universe and Savior of all mankind. What a glorious day that will be! I hope to see you in that glad throng.

Chapter 11

See the FATHER

Now, I challenge you to see the Father. When His EYES were revealed, He was showing us that He was looking the world over to find those who were willing to accept His love. Look into His eyes. See His desire for you. See His longing. See His devotion. He is looking your way.

When His EARS were revealed, He was showing us that He has time for a personal audience. His EARS are still open to hear your faintest responses to His call. He hears your every petition, and He is eagerly listening for your words of praise.

When His FACE was revealed, He was showing us that His countenance is available to change us from what we are to what we can become. He can change all that has disappointed us and caused us to be dissatisfied and unashamed. He wants us to come FACE to FACE with His presence, as Jacob did at Jabbok and

Peniel. There He will settle all our fears, erase all our doubts, and confirm to us His greatness. Don't turn away from Him.

When His MOUTH was revealed, He was letting us know what was in His heart: purity, cleanliness, justice, wholesomeness and righteousness. He was showing us that He is a God of communication, that He always has spoken and always will speak to those who are willing to listen and obey His words. Stop for a minute right now. Listen for His voice. He wants to speak to you today.

When His MIND was revealed, He was showing us His wonderful design for everything that has been created. He understands all things, knows all things, and controls all things. He has all wisdom and never has to second-guess a situation. His thoughts are so much higher than our own. He knows exactly what He is doing. We should trust Him more. He loves us and has our best interests at heart.

When His HEART was revealed, He was showing us what He is really like and how He really feels. He showed us that His most prized creation, the only thing worthy of redemption, was the soul of man and that He was willing to sacrifice His Only Son to guarantee our salvation. He was showing us that His is a giving Heart, one that keeps on giving, even when there is little or no response on our part; for in that center of God is found the purest and most potent fountain of love and devotion ever imagined. Hear the cry of His heart today.

When His ARM was revealed, He was showing us His strength and His willingness to manifest that strength on our behalf. He was saying to us that He is fully able to provide for and protect those who love Him. He showed us that His ARMS are outstretched to us and long to draw us near to Him. Don't disappoint Him by refusing His offer.

When His HAND was revealed, HE was assuring us of His care and support. He was reminding us of His sacrifice. He was teaching us that His power is all-encompassing and engulfing, that His HANDS are mighty—for blessing or for chastening.

When His FINGER was revealed, He was assuring us of His ability to separate us from the oppressor, just as He did for the children of Israel when they suffered under the heavy hand of the Pharaoh in Egypt. He wants us to know that His fingers fly to accomplish the goal He always has in mind. And He wants us to know that His offer to miraculously write with His FINGER the law of God upon our hearts still stands.

When His FEET were revealed, we learned that He has always been in control, that He is not about to be conquered by any enemy—be it man or devil. We saw that He will soon put all enemies, once and for all, UNDER HIS FEET and UNDER OUR FEET. What a great God we serve! Yield your life to Him today so that you can obtain the glorious destiny He has prepared for you!

Index of References

1. From National Geographic News, *Encyclopedia of 7700 Illustrations,* (Rockville, MD: Assurance Publishers, 1979), pp. 1244

2. R. Laird Harris, Gleason L. Archer, Sr., Bruce K. Waltke, *Theological Workbook of the Old Testament,* (Chicago: Moody Press, 1980), 2:663

3. *The Ear Shape Shows Personality, Encyclopedia of 7700 Illustrations,* (Rockville, MD: Assurance Publishers, 1979), pp. 744

4. Francis Brown, S.R. Driver, Charles A. Briggs, *A Hebrew and English Lexicon of the Old Testament,* (Oxford: Clarendon Press, 1951), pp. 24

5. *Oh I Want to See Him* by R.H. Cornelius, Copyright © 1944, Renewal by Melodies of Praise (Springfield, MO: Gospel Publishing House, 1957, pp. 93

6. R. Laird Harris, Gleason L. Archer, Sr., Bruce K. Waltke, *Theological Workbook of the Old Testament,* (Chicago: Moody Press, 1980), 2:727

7. *The Lighted Face of Judson* by Mrs. Ruby Miller, *Encyclopedia of 7700 Illustrations,* (Rockville, MD: Assurance Publishers, 1979), pp. 680-681

8. R. Laird Harris, Gleason L. Archer, Sr., Bruce K. Waltke, *Theological Workbook of the Old Testament,* (Chicago: Moody Press, 1980), 2:718

9. *Heart Break, Encyclopedia of 7700 Illustrations,* (Rockville, MD: Assurance Publishers, 1979), pp. 543

10. *Create Him* by J.A. Clarks, *Encyclopedia of 7700 Illustrations,* (Rockville, MD: Assurance Publishers, 1979), pp. 493

11. *God Moves In Mysterious Ways, Encyclopedia of 7700 Illustrations,* (Rockville, MD: Assurance Publishers, 1979), pp. 494

12. *Text Is Too Big, Encyclopedia of 7700 Illustrations,* (Rockville, MD: Assurance Publishers, 1979), pp. 496

13. *Love In 3 Dimensions, Encyclopedia of 7700 Illustrations,* (Rockville, MD: Assurance Publishers, 1979), pp. 496

14. *Gospel In Miniature, Encyclopedia of 7700 Illustrations,* (Rockville, MD: Assurance Publishers, 1979), pp. 496

15. Walter Bauer, William F. Arnd and F. Wilbur Gingrich, *A Greek-English Lexicon of the New Testament,* (Chicago: University of Chicago Press, 1979), pp. 65

16. The New International Dictionary of New Testament Theology, Vol.2. p. 149. Regency Reference Library, Zondervan Publishing House, Grand Rapids, MI. Colin Brown, Gen. Editor. 1981

17. *Durer's Praying Hands,* from *The Bible Friend, Encyclopedia of 7700 Illustrations,* (Rockville, MD: Assurance Publishers, 1979), pp. 463

18. *Giving Her Right Hand, Encyclopedia of 7700 Illustrations,* (Rockville, MD: Assurance Publishers, 1979), pp. 575

19. *Sympathetic Jewel by A.C. Price, Encyclopedia of 7700 Illustrations,* (Rockville, MD: Assurance Publishers, 1979), pp. 677

20. *Charlemagne's Position After Death, Encyclopedia of 7700 Illustrations,* (Rockville, MD: Assurance Publishers, 1979), pp. 1213-1214

About the Author

Jim McAtee was raised in Oklahoma City and after graduation from high school, spent the next three years in the U.S. Army where he served a year in the Islamic country of Turkey. After his service duty, he returned home and attended Bethany Nazarene College, Bethany, Oklahoma and later received a bachelors degree from Central Bible College in Springfield, Missouri in 1967.

He and his wife Bonnie have three daughters and now reside in Sanford, Maine where he has been pastoring since 1976. Jim is a member of Rotary International and is active in serving on various volunteer boards in civil government.

Sparked by a strong desire to help people understand how personable God is, this work in an attempt to convey the concepts and experiences to other seekers in an effort to help them find a meaningful relationship with the Almighty and His Son, Jesus Christ. God is indeed a "rewarder of them that diligently search for Him." As defined in the Word, as "Love" and "A Spirit", the Word also declares to man that He is convincingly more.

Jim has a burden for the third world countries and has done some teaching and evangelistic ministry in the country of India.

As we prepare to enter the 21st Century, God is seeking for a people to "know Him", in word and above all, in practice.